CAROLINE WREY'S
SECRETS FOR
SUCCESSFUL
ENTERTAINING

CAROLINE WREY'S
SECRETS FOR
SUCCESSFUL
ENTERTAINING

HOW TO BE A PERFECT HOSTESS

COLLINS & BROWN

I want to dedicate this book to George, who is the most gorgeous husband, father and host. We are all devoted to him.

First published in Great Britain in 2000
by Collins & Brown Limited
64 Brewery Road
London
N7 9NT

A member of the Chrysalis Group plc

9 8 7 6 5 4 3 2

British Library Cataloguing-in-Publication Data:
A catalogue record for this book is available from the British Library.

ISBN 1 85585 973 4

Conceived, edited and designed by Collins & Brown Limited

Editor: Kate Haxell
Designer: Janet James
Interior, project and lifestyle photography: Lucinda Symons
Food, step-by-step and additional photography: Brian Hatton
Stylist: Alistair Turnbull
Illustrations: Dominic Harris

Reproduction by Global Colour
Printed and bound by Paramount Printing Company, Hong Kong

Distributed in the United States and Canada by Sterling Publishing Co,
387 Park Avenue South, New York, NY 10016, USA

contents

introduction

Entertaining, on any scale, is huge fun and 'giving' is as good as receiving, if not better. I love holding parties, as they are a perfect ploy to see family and friends whom I love, or people I would love to know better. But the whole enterprise must be as easy and pleasurable as possible. It's no fun if it is stressful and difficult.

In this book we cater for several different events, from a formal dinner to a teenage sleepover. These occasions have in common several elements that are important in entertaining successfully. Each chapter looks at elements of planning an occasion, but the ideas are also relevant to other events, so do consult any or all of them. Above all, plan the mix of people so they will enjoy one another's company: it's lovely when your friends like each other and become friends, too.

Some guests sit and chat after dinner, whereas others love to play party games. Children cannot be expected to sit chatting; they must be allowed to get down and do their own thing, or something organized by you. Either way, they are your guests and you must bear them in mind when planning the event.

Brilliant food is of paramount importance, of course: there must be a huge emphasis on the colour, taste and texture of all that you offer. It must be very, very delicious, but it can still be fairly simple. Good presentation is vital – it simply 'makes' the meal. Throughout this book there are pages of ideas for menus, food presentation and easy recipes for all occasions.

Tablecloths, napkins, napkin rings, bed linens, jug covers, wine coasters and, of course, flowers, all add special touches to the overall atmosphere you are trying to create. With this in mind, every chapter in the book offers projects to make the occasion special. Again, many are interchangeable, so do experiment.

No matter what the occasion, with a little effort and creativity it can be made wonderful for everyone involved.

Carole Wray

Lunches and Dinners

Lunch and dinner parties offer an unrivalled opportunity to produce delicious food for friends and family, whether it be at a picnic or at a more formal occasion.

As the host or hostess, it is part of your job to make sure that everyone is happy and has met the other guests. At a seated dinner a simple way to ensure that everyone talks to everyone is to move all the girls round two places to the left after the third course. On less formal occasions people will mingle more naturally and you can just make appropriate introductions.

In this chapter we look at a romantic supper for two, a family picnic on the beach, a Christmas lunch, a formal dinner party and an outdoor lunch. Each occasion is orientated towards quite different people and has quite different priorities. So we have devised an easy-to-serve menu for you and a special someone, and practical accessories for a perfect picnic. There are glittering Christmas decorations, a simple guide to making a dining table look wonderful and some seriously summery salads.

Romantic
Supper

Either the kitchen or the dining room can be the setting for a romantic, cosy supper, though if you choose the kitchen do make sure it is tidy: a screen is a brilliant way of hiding any unromantic piles of washing-up.

To set the scene you need to create the perfect atmosphere, which means getting the details right. The presence of a tablecloth creates instant elegance; padded seat covers on the chairs transform their look and add to comfort; monogramming the table napkins makes the whole thing so very personal. Candles are deeply romantic, especially when used in abundance: create a forest of lit candles for your special guest to walk into. Perfumed oil-burners are good, but the scent must be extremely subtle or it could interfere with the smell and taste of the food – which will, of course, be sublime.

Creating
the Right Atmosphere

You want to have everything completely ready and organized, so that when your special guest arrives they will sense an atmosphere of warmth and romance. Don't leave things until the last minute, or you will feel stressed and overwhelmed, with too much to do in too little time – this will take all the pleasure out of the preparation, which is so special. I love it when people are ten minutes late, though you can't count on this. Thinking ahead means you will have plenty of time for vital things such as a bath, hair, nails, make-up and clothes.

Decorating the Table

Buy your flowers at least two days in advance, as this will give them a chance to open, but also allow you time to arrange them to their best advantage. Lilies can take days to open but, when they do, their aroma is sensational. Conversely, lilies that are still uncooperatively green and closed look terribly depressing. If you choose to put an arrangement on the table, make it low and not too large, so that it does not get in the way.

A monogrammed table napkin is a beautiful, deeply personal detail, which cannot fail to touch your dining partner (see page 16). Hand-stitching a single letter, and adding the odd bead to give the letter some sparkle, is so quick and simple to do. I always love to have something that can be sewn on my lap in the evening in front of a good television programme. But if you have a very clever sewing machine, you can always use the satin stitch on it to create your letter (though you will need to back it with removable interfacing to avoid any puckering). You can place the napkin as it is on the table, or tie it with a luxurious ribbon that matches the colour of the initial. A tablecloth is a must, and your best cutlery, china and glass to add to the special atmosphere.

Preparing the Room

Make sure that the room looks lovely, with everything in its place and no unsightly piles of newspapers or dusty surfaces. Close the curtains and use table or standard lamps and candles, rather than the brilliant glare of an overhead bulb, to light the room. If you have a fire, either a real one or a flame-effect one, do light it. Put on some music; a classical instrumental piece always makes good background music for conversation.

The padded, tufted cushions (see page 17) are obviously quite a large project, but they will add to your guest's comfort and, once done, they can live conveniently in a cupboard, ready to be brought out for special occasions only.

- Check the room temperature.
- Flowers should be sweet-smelling.
- Clean table linen.
- China and glasses.
- Perfumed oil-burner.
- Candles.
- Light the fire.
- Close the curtains.
- Music.

checklist

Far left: embroider your napkins in a colour to suit the other furnishings in the room.

Left above: roses may be a romantic favourite, but they are always beautiful.

Left: a scented candle provides both light and a subtle perfume.

FISH PIE

Ask your fishmonger to skin and de-bone 200g (7oz) each of white fish and smoked haddock. Place the fish in an ovenproof dish, cover with 500ml (18fl oz, 2 cups) of milk and bake for 25min at 180°C/350°F/ gas mark 4. In a large saucepan, melt 30g (1¼oz, ⅛ cup) butter, add 30g (1¼oz, ¼ cup) of flour and stir on the heat for 1min. Off the heat, pour on the milk from the fish dish. Blend. Return to the heat and stir until thick. Break up the fish with a fork, checking for any bones. Stir the fish into the sauce with 200g (7oz) of prawns, 2 hardboiled eggs (shelled and chopped), seasoning and parsley. You can also add the juice of a lemon or a sprinkling of cayenne pepper if you wish. Pour the mixture back into the dish and cover it with 3 heaped tbsp of white breadcrumbs. Bake at 180°C/350°F/gas mark 4 for 25min if cold from the fridge or, if straight from the preparation stage, for 15min.

STRIPED ZUCCHINI

Top and tail your zucchini (courgettes). Stripe their skin, with 1cm (½in) gaps between stripes, using the sharp side of a citrus zester. Now cut them into thin slices and steam them for 7min. They can be prepared in advance and the water set to boil before you sit down. Put the zucchini on to cook when you take in the starter plates. By the time you have taken the main dish to the table, they will be ready.

An Easy-to-Serve Menu

On this occasion you do not want to spend a long time in the kitchen either before or during supper. Thus it is worth planning your menu accordingly. This will obviously vary according to the seasons but here is a perfect one. As a starter serve a combination of grilled vegetables and mozzarella. Once prepared, this can be grilled for three minutes under a hot grill and garnished with parsley before serving. Fish pie is an excellent main course that can be made a day in advance and cooked through at the last minute. Alternatively, boeuf bourgignon can be made up to four days before. Serve either of them with new potatoes, which can be kept warm, and striped zucchini, which cook quickly. Pot au chocolat is a delicious pudding that can be made four days ahead and kept in the fridge or deep freeze. Small details like extra-special coffee or herbal tea are important. Also, don't forget to chill or open wine well in advance and to have a box of matches ready to hand for the candles.

POT AU CHOCOLAT
Put 3 packets of plain-chocolate polka dots in a food processor. Put a little water in a saucepan, pour it out but do not dry the pan (this ensures that the cream won't catch on the base, which makes it hard to wash up). Pour 600ml (1pt, 2½ cups) of thin cream into the pan and heat until nearly boiling, but do not boil. Pour the cream over the polka dots, put on the lid and switch on the machine, the polka dots will melt instantly. Add 3 eggs through the feed tube and process until combined. Pour out into ramekins and chill in the fridge for at least 1hr.

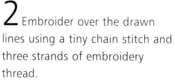

materials

Napkin

Vanishing pen

Skein of six-stranded embroidery thread

Embroidery needle

Tiny glass beads to match thread

Beading needle

Monogrammed Napkin

Monogramming a table napkin for someone special must be the ultimate personal touch. No one could fail to notice such a detail – and if they did you would just have to point it out to them. This type of hand embroidery uses one of the easiest of stitches; you could do this by machine but it really would not be quite the same.

1 Using the vanishing pen, draw a letter on a corner of the napkin. We have drawn quite an elaborate one with little curls at the ends. If you are confident of your calligraphic skills, draw the letter straight on to the fabric with the vanishing pen. Alternatively, draw the letter out with a pencil on plain paper first. Then tape the paper to a window and tape the fabric over it so that the letter is in the right position. Trace over the lines of the letter on to the fabric with the vanishing pen.

2 Embroider over the drawn lines using a tiny chain stitch and three strands of embroidery thread.

3 Using one strand of embroidery thread and the beading needle, stitch a tiny glass bead into each curl of the letter.

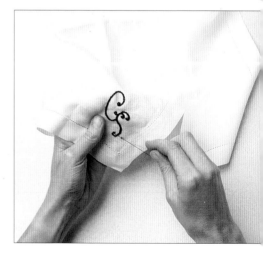

Tufted Cushion

This looks fantastic – so very sumptuous and inviting. The basic shape is easy to make, but the tufts and buttons require a small pair of pliers. Without these, pulling the wool through the feather pad becomes a very hard task indeed. As my chair was shaped, I narrowed the back of the fabric cover to fit it; there is no need to narrow the pad itself.

materials

Rectangle of fabric measuring 53 x 103cm (21 x 41in)

Long ruler

Pins

Scissors

Sewing machine

Matching sewing threads

80cm (32in) of matching bias binding

Cushion pad measuring 50 x 50cm (20 x 20in)

Sewing needle

8m (8yd) embroidery wool

Long, sharp darning needle

Polyester button thread to match wool

8 covered buttons

1 Right sides facing, fold the fabric in half lengthways. On the raw short side (which will be the back), measure in 5cm (2in) from each edge and mark with a pin. Cut a slanting, straight line through both layers, from the folded edge to the pin.

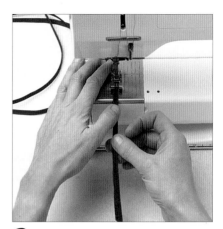

2 Fold the bias binding in half widthways and machine close to the edge. Cut it into two 40cm (16in) lengths and neaten the ends.

3 Fold one piece of binding in half and pin the fold to the raw back edge 2cm (¾in) in from the side. Do the same with the other piece of binding on the other side.

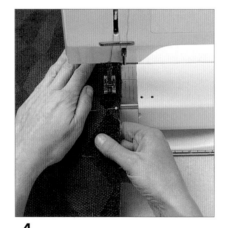

4 Machine up each side from the fold to the back corner, then round the corner and along the back 5cm (2in). Turn right side out.

5 Insert the cushion into the cover, making sure that the corners of the pad fill out the corners of the cover. Slip stitch the gap closed.

6 For each tuft, cut 1m (1yd) of embroidery wool and thread up a needle. Wind the wool ten times around two fingers.

7 Slip the bundle off your fingers and tightly bind the loose end four times round the middle of the bundle, creating a bow shape. Make two stitches to secure the tuft by pushing the needle through the back of the binding loops. Leave the long end of wool attached to the tuft.

8 To strengthen the tail of wool, cut a length of polyester button thread twice the length of the tail of the tuft. Fold it in half and loop it over the centre of the tuft. Smooth the ends of the thread and the tail of wool together.

9 Plan the spacing of the tufts and buttons following any pattern on the fabric, or spacing them evenly if the fabric is plain. Thread a very long needle with the free end of wool and polyester threads of a tuft. Push the needle into the cushion where the tuft will sit, then right through the cushion and out where the button will sit. You will find this easier if you push the point of the needle through, then grab this with a pair of pliers and use these to pull the wool through the pad.

10 Take the needle through the shank of the covered button, then back down through the cushion again.

11 Bring the needle out in the middle of the tuft. Secure the wool by taking the needle twice through the binding loops of the tuft.

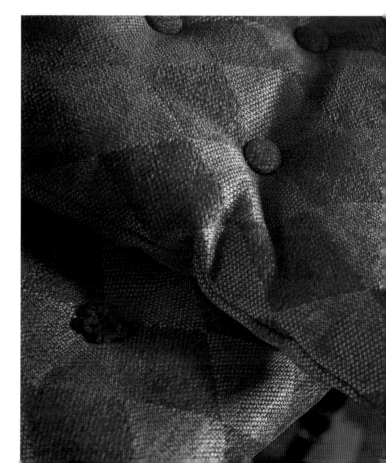

CHAPTER TWO

The Perfect Picnic

Whether you go out to the countryside or down to the sea, picnics are such fun to plan: all that delicious food, pretty hampers with all their practical contents and the essential rug. I love to go on beach picnics, especially to rocky beaches where there are plenty of rockpools for the children to fish in but no sand to get in your food.

You often have a real mix of ages at a picnic, resulting in a similarly varied mix of interests. The adults will adore fascinating and colourful food, whereas most children are far more gripped by going netting in rockpools, damning streams or catching tiny fish. For them the picnic food must be easily eaten with their fingers and should be accompanied by lots of drinks. But for the adults the greater the variety of food you can present on pretty plastic plates, the better.

Far left and left: rockpools and streams will provide hours of entertainment for children of all ages.

Below: the simplest salad looks most appetizing presented on a colourful plastic plate.

Planning a Picnic

For comfort on damp ground or rough rocks you have to take a rug on a picnic. Making a rug from an old blanket (the perfect thickness) is very practical and uses up a blanket that would otherwise clutter up the linen cupboard (see page 26). A hamper is such a good idea for transporting and serving food from at a picnic. Lining it not only makes it look extremely attractive, but also cushions the contents and stops them rattling around too much (see page 24).

It's very nice to be handed a cutlery wrap at a picnic with everything you need inside (see page 28). Wraps also make it easy for the hostess to make sure that the right number of knives, forks, spoons and napkins has been packed and the wraps travel easily in the hamper. Square and rectangular plastic boxes take up less room than round ones and plastic jars or bottles weigh less than glass ones.

Perfect Picnic Food

There are many priorities for picnic food: there is no point in having food that will melt on a hot day, and, equally, no point taking stuff that is heavy to carry or hard to cut. A mixture of finger and fork food is very practical. Many people love chicken legs (wrap the ends in foil to prevent greasy fingers), grilled sausages and delicious bread. Long-leafed lettuce and chicory are good for dipping in mayonnaise, as are carrot sticks, cucumber sticks and cherry tomatoes. It's lovely if you can cook the chicken and sausages near to the time of departure, since both are so good warm. Any kind of soup would be good on a cool day – preferably a

home-made one, but most people seem to like tinned tomato soup if you run out of time – it really warms everyone up. Take enough plastic mugs to serve it in.

Apart from the meat, soup and salad, the picnic can be prepared and packed the night before. If it is really hot weather, it is worth freezing plastic (never glass) bottles of water to take, so that they remain extremely cold throughout the day.

Having eaten all those savoury things, something sweet is most welcome. A loaf-shaped fruitcake travels and cuts well and has a wholesome, old-fashioned taste. Plastic boxes full of strawberries, cherries and cut-up nectarines also go down well. If it is an all-day picnic I always make sure there is something deliciously different for the afternoon and a thermos of boiling water for a cup of tea. Keep small, plastic screw-top jars full of coffee, tea and sugar in your hamper throughout the summer so that they are always there and don't need to be remembered every time. Equally, leave two empty plastic carrier bags in the hamper, one for the dirty cutlery, plates and mugs and one for any leftover food: this makes clearing up on the beach so easy.

Entertainment for All

If you are going to a rockpool beach take nets, as children love to search for tiny fish and crabs. Make sure there is one net and one bucket per child to avoid friction. Take a seashore book so that they can identify everything they catch. Do make sure that you put all the sealife back in the pools before leaving the beach so that the creatures can continue to live happily.

Buckets and spades will lead to fantastic castle-building, while a football, Frisbee, kite, cricket or badminton set will occupy people of all ages for hours.

If you can drive right up to your picnic spot, perhaps at a school or sporting event, a table and chairs are added luxuries. Also, pretty flowers in a non-spill jam-jar vase add such style to your picnic. On a workbench, with a hammer and screwdriver, punch holes through the lid, from the outside in. Fill the jar three-quarters full with water then screw the lid back on and arrange the flowers through the holes in the lid.

Above: make your own non-spill vase and fill it with garden flowers to make your picnic table extra smart.

Left: rich fruit cake, made with lots of dried fruit, is a tasty – and very practical – picnic pudding.

- Food must be practical to transport and easy to eat.

- Glasses, cutlery and plates must be unbreakable and very lightweight.

- Enough baskets to carry everything.

- Blanket to sit on.

- Plastic bags for packing up.

- Nets, plastic containers, seashore books and wellington boots for children.

- Games for adults and children.

- Binoculars for those people interested in spotting seabirds.

checklist

Quilted Picnic Hamper Liner

Choose a thin fabric that doesn't fray easily for the hamper liner. Doing the quilting by hand means you have some lovely therapeutic hand-sewing to do in the evening. The little ties are essential to hold the liner in place and a separate quilted 'lid' will help to stop items from rattling about and breaking.

materials

Tape measure

Paper

Pencil

Two pieces of fabric large enough to fit your hamper; our pieces measured 75 x 100cm (29½ x 39in)

Scissors

Pins

Matching sewing threads

Sewing machine

Iron

One piece of 50g (2oz) synthetic wadding the same size as the fabric

One skein of six-stranded embroidery thread or yarn

Embroidery needle

4m (160in) of 1cm- (½in-) wide ribbon

Sewing needle

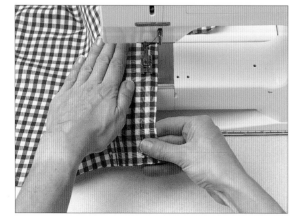

1 Measure the inside of your hamper and draw a paper pattern following the diagram opposite. Add a 1cm (½in) seam allowance all round, then cut two pieces of fabric to size. Right sides facing, machine the two pieces together. Starting on a short side, 5cm (2in) from a corner, machine round the edges, finishing on the side you started on, 5cm (2in) in from the other corner. Leave the central part of this side open.

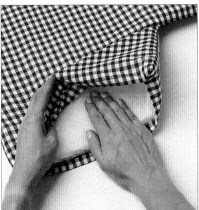

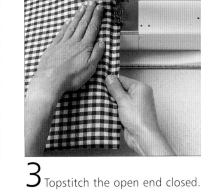

2 Clip the corners, turn the liner right side out and press, ensuring that the raw edges of the open end are pressed under. Cut the wadding to the same size as the liner, then slip the wadding in through the open end of the liner, making sure it reaches right into the corners.

3 Topstitch the open end closed.

4 Decide how you would like to quilt the liner. As we used a check, we simply made a quilting knot at every tenth square. On a plain fabric the knots should be approximately every 7cm ($2\frac{3}{4}$in). Thread the needle with a length of embroidery thread or yarn, using all six strands. Take the needle down through all the layers of fabric and wadding, then bring it up again just beside the insertion point. Pull the thread through, leaving a 5cm (2in) tail of thread.

5 Tie the ends of thread in a firm double knot and cut them 1cm ($\frac{1}{2}$in) above the knot to make a little tuft.

To make a quilted 'lid' to go inside your hamper, measure the top and cut two pieces of fabric and a piece of wadding to size. Right sides facing, machine them together, leaving a gap as before, then turn right side out and insert the wadding. Quilt the 'lid' as described in steps 4 and 5.

6 Cut a 50cm (20in) length of ribbon and sew the centre of it to a corner of the hamper liner. Repeat on each of the outer corners so that there are eight ties in total. Fit the liner into the hamper, thread the ribbons through the top edge of the wickerwork and tie them in neat bows.

Right: use this diagram as a guide when measuring your picnic hamper and cutting a paper pattern for the quilted liner.

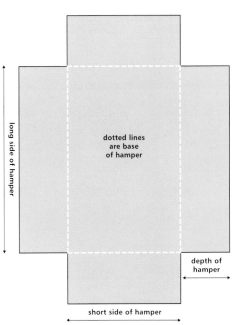

long side of hamper

dotted lines are base of hamper

depth of hamper

short side of hamper

Seaside Picnic Rug

You can cut out any felt shapes you like for this project: it just happens that these ones suited our beach theme. It is really worth backing the rug with waterproof fabric, because the ground can be damp; a thin groundsheet from a camping shop is ideal. Blankets and groundsheets are quite heavy, so use a denim needle when you are machining the binding to the edge.

materials

Starfish template on page 124

Felt

Scissors

Old blanket with any edging cut off

Pins

One skein of six-stranded embroidery thread

Waterproof backing fabric, the same size as the blanket

5cm- (2in-) wide ribbon measuring twice the length and twice the width of the blanket, plus 10cm (4in)

Matching sewing threads

Sewing machine

1 Enlarge the starfish template to the required size and cut it out. Draw round it on to felt and cut out the shape. Cut out as many as you need.

2 Position the starfish on the blanket: if there are any worn patches on the blanket, cover them up with starfish. Appliqué them to the blanket with evenly spaced running stitches.

3 Pin the waterproof backing to the blanket around all four edges. The easiest way to do this is to spread the blanket out face-down on the floor, then lay the backing on top of it and pin the two layers together along the edges.

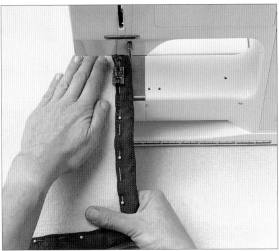

4 Fold the ribbon in half over the edge of the blanket and backing, around all four edges. Pin it in position as you go, using the pins holding the backing to the fabric. Machine close to the edge all round, mitring each corner.

Rectangle of fabric measuring
52 x 56cm (21 x 22¾in) for
the wrap

Iron

Rectangle of heavy, fusible
interfacing measuring
25 x 54cm (10 x 21¾in)

Pins

Sewing machine

Matching sewing threads

Rectangle of fabric measuring
14 x 16cm (5½ x 6¼in) for
the pocket

100cm (39in) of 3.5cm-
(1⅜in-) wide ribbon

Cutlery Wrap

These are very easy to make as you are
merely working with two rectangles of
fabric, some ribbon and some
interfacing. The project comes together
with such speed and ease and will really
complement the picnic hamper as well
as the whole picnic. Wraps also provide
a lovely excuse to incorporate some truly
stunning ribbon into a project.

1 Press under 1cm (½in) all round the wrap piece of fabric. Fit the fusible interfacing (sticky-side down) under the pressed-under edges on one half of the fabric. Iron it with a hot iron to fuse it to the fabric.

2 Fold the fabric in half over the interfacing. Machine the two halves together, working close to the pressed edge. The stiffened side will be the back of the wrap.

3 Press under 1cm (½in) around all four edges of the pocket piece of fabric. Machine across the top edge. Pin the pocket in position on the front of the wrap: it should be on the right-hand side, approximately 3cm (1¼in) in from the right-hand edge and 4cm (1½in) up from the bottom edge. Machine it to the wrap down each side and across the bottom.

4 Turn the wrap over so that you are working on the back. Fold the length of ribbon in half and press the fold to crease it. Lay the crease on the stitching line in the centre of the right-hand side of the wrap and machine across it three times to hold it firmly. Put your cutlery and napkin into the pocket, roll the wrap up and tie it with the ribbon.

CHAPTER THREE

Christmas Lunch

This is one of the most important family occasions of the whole year. I look forward to it, and all its delightful details, enormously. Preparing both the Christmas table and the food, with all your family helping you, is so creative and deeply satisfying. Once done, everything should be a feast for the eyes. All that delicious Christmas food deserves to be set against the background of a beautiful table, covered with festive decorations to compose a fantastic overall picture of warmth, welcome, celebration and enjoyment.

It is just such fun if everyone is involved in the production of the Christmas goodies. Children love painting with gold or silver paints and making sequinned fruit. Although the table-mats will take you a little time to make, you can use them year after year and derive the same degree of pleasure every time.

Setting the Christmas Table

It's just not possible to start making your Christmas decorations too early. They need be neither viewed nor displayed until late December, but to get them done in good time is marvellous. I like to have a simple colour scheme for Christmas, so I make everything in gold and white to complement white china and gold-stemmed glasses.

Do begin making the appliquéd tablemats in good time because they will take a little more work than the other projects (see page 36). You may well have in your fabric bag a lovely selection of remnants that could be used to make mats, or you can have a field day selecting stunning fabrics, ribbons and trimmings from your favourite fabric shop. It's fun to involve your children in all the exciting choices. You could make all your appliquéd mats to match, or have two themes, or else make each one totally different. I like to have mine all the same, as I love the elegance a matching set gives to the table. However, for a more colourful look, different mats are what you need.

You don't need an expensive sewing machine to do appliqué work; one capable of a simple satin stitch is all that is required. Iron-on interfacing is essential so that your fabrics will not pucker. Back the whole tablemat in something sturdy – heavy cotton is ideal. It's important that all the fabrics you use can withstand both washing and hot plates.

Table Decorations

Making sequinned fruit to sit in a basket for the table-centre decoration is very creative (see page 38). It is amazing how much children of all ages enjoy this activity. Polystyrene shapes are a perfect base for a

Left: tiny gold stars in gilded terracotta coasters add an extra festive detail to the table.
Above: if your Christmas tree is in the dining room, decorate it in the same colours that you have used on the table for a very stylish overall look.

successful end result. If you wanted to, you could cut leaves out of gold organza and pin them on to the tops of the fruit. Paint walnuts with gold spray-paint and sit them among the fruit – any activity involving gold paint is always fun and instantly rewarding. Use a gold or sparkly voile or tissue as a lining for the basket, to give it warmth and softness.

Finishing Touches

An over-cloth of gold voile on a white tablecloth looks absolutely beautiful and a tassel at each corner is the perfect way of holding down such a light piece of fabric. No festive table is complete without candlesticks and tying a fine, trailing ribbon to each one adds a truly decorative quality to the table. Tie your napkins with the same or similar ribbons. Your candlesticks should frame your glorious sequinned centrepiece, which should not be too high, so everyone can see across the table. Buy very tall, non-drip candles for your candlesticks and replace them when they come close to the ribbons. Also, make sure all your decorations leave enough room on the table for serving platters and sauces.

All of these details can be recreated in different colours and designs for other occasions: use yellow and green for Easter, or favourite colours to suit a particular birthday or special celebration.

- China and cutlery – enough place settings for the number of guests.
- Tablecloth and over-cloth to complement your china and cutlery.
- Mats that are both heat- and wash-proof.
- A table-centre decoration that is not too tall.
- Candlesticks, ribbons and non-drip candles.
- Napkins, and ribbons to tie them with.
- Enough space on the table for all the serving platters.

checklist

Above: small tassels, the kind used to trim soft furnishings, not only add a decorative touch to an over-cloth, but help to hold it in place.
Left: if you are using organza ribbon to tie your napkins, choose a wired variety, as it much easier to tie this type into full, rounded bows.

ALMOND PRALINE
Dissolve 75g (3oz, ⅓ cup) of caster sugar in a little water. Bring to the boil, but do not stir or it will turn cloudy. Watch it carefully, as it burns very easily, and when it is a pale, golden brown, throw in 175g (6oz, 1 cup) of roasted almonds, whole or sliced. Turn the mixture out on to an oiled marble or metal surface. When it is cold, break it into small pieces.

Home-made
Sweets

Home-made chocolates or sweets are the perfect finish to a wonderful Christmas lunch or dinner. They look so pretty on the table and taste divine. To present each kind in different way makes them look particularly inviting. The tiny cinnamon meringues, which are very fragile, look mouth-watering when presented in little paper cases or cellophane wrappers, which can also be used like tiny crackers to decorate the tree.

Chocolate squares, truffles and praline look sumptuous in a tiny container like a ramekin dish, a basket or decorative paper cases. You or your children can make them in advance, as part of the build-up to Christmas. However, don't let younger children make praline, as the caramel can burn both itself and them. The chocolate-based sweets freeze splendidly while nut and meringue ones live happily for months in an airtight container. It is worth making different varieties, as then you cater for all different tastes.

CHOCOLATE SQUARES

Crumb 18 sweet wholemeal biscuits in a food processor. Melt 24 small squares of very good-quality, plain chocolate in a bowl over a pan of boiling water. Stir 200ml (7fl oz, ⅔ cup) of heavy cream and the biscuit crumbs into the melted chocolate. Spread the mixture out over a greased metal tray. Chill in the fridge until firm. Dust with caster sugar and cut into very small squares.

CINNAMON MERINGUES

(makes about 30 depending on size)

Grease two large baking trays. Whisk 4 egg whites with a pinch of salt until they form peaks. Mix 225g (8oz, 1 cup) of sugar and 2 tbsp of ground cinnamon together, then sprinkle a spoonful at a time into the eggs, whisking thoroughly between each addition. Keep whisking until all the sugar is combined and the mixture stands in firm peaks. Pipe meringues on to the baking trays from a piping bag with a decorative nozzle. Bake for 1½ hr at 130°C/250°F/gas mark ½.

CHOCOLATE TRUFFLES

Melt 225g (8oz, 8 squares) of dark chocolate with 1 level tsp of instant coffee dissolved in 1tbsp of boiling water. Remove the pan from the heat and beat in 100g (4oz, ½ cup) of butter, then a few drops of brandy. Put the mixture in the fridge to harden. Roll small balls of it into truffles in your hands then drop them into cocoa powder. Store them in the fridge or freezer.

Appliquéd Table-mat

These are utterly gorgeous and every time you lay the table with them they will give you huge, renewed pleasure. They are not quick to make, but are so worth all the time and effort invested in them. I always soak them and then wash them by hand, out of respect to the appliqué work, rather than consigning them to the washing machine.

materials

Two rectangles of fabric measuring 32 x 42cm (13 x 15in), one for the front and one for the back of the mat

One rectangle of medium-weight interfacing measuring 32 x 42cm (13 x 15in)

Tree template on page 124

One square of gold net measuring 25 x 15cm (10 x 6in)

One rectangle of tissue paper measuring 25 x 15cm (10 x 6in)

Scissors

Gold sewing thread

Sewing machine

One square of gold fabric measuring 25 x 15cm (10 x 6in)

One square of fusible webbing measuring 25 x 15cm (10 x 6in)

Iron

Gold embroidery thread

Sharp embroidery needle

150cm (59in) of 5cm- (2in-) wide gold ribbon

1 Pin the rectangle of interfacing to the back of the front rectangle of fabric, placing a pin at each corner.

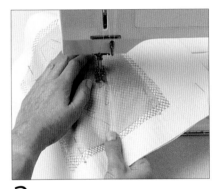

2 Enlarge the tree template to the required size. Trace it on to tissue paper and lay this on the gold net. Lay the net and tissue in position on the mat. Using gold thread and a small, straight stitch, machine round the tree outline, stitching through all the layers.

3 Gently pull the tissue paper away from the stitches.

4 Trim away the excess netting to reveal the tree shape. Cut close to the stitching but be careful not to cut through it.

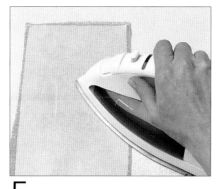

5 Iron the fusible webbing on to the back of the gold fabric. It is advisable to test this out on a scrap piece first to check that the heat of the iron does not damage the fabric.

6 Draw round the tree template on to the backing paper of the webbing and cut out the shape.

7 Peel the paper backing off the webbing, position the gold tree on the mat and iron it in place.

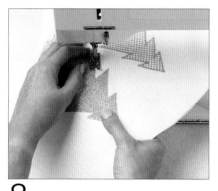

8 Using a small, tight satin stitch, machine right round both the trees, enclosing all the raw edges.

9 Embroider stars across the white fabric in gold embroidery thread. The stars are made up of eight straight stitches, each coming up through the fabric at the outer point and going back down through the centre. If you have a computerized sewing machine, you may be able to program it to stitch these stars for you.

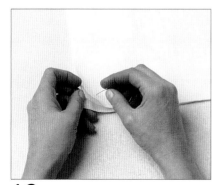

10 Remove the corner pins and turn the mat over. Pin the back rectangle of fabric to the mat, aligning the raw edges.

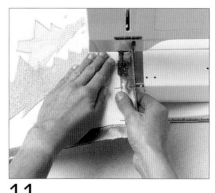

11 Fold the gold ribbon in half over the edge of the mat around all sides and pin it in position. Using a small zigzag stitch and gold sewing thread, machine the ribbon to the mat all round, catching both sides in the stitching. Mitre the corners as you machine round.

Polystyrene fruit form

Pen

Gold and silver sequins

Gold and silver pins

0.3cm- (⅛in-) wide silver ribbon, measuring four times the length of the fruit form

Gold or silver glass-headed pin

Gold or silver filigree

Sequinned Fruit Table Centre

Although these fruits are not quick projects, they can be made on your lap almost anywhere. Children really enjoy making them and they are very forgiving of mistakes, though, as they involve pins, the fruits are not suitable projects for very small children. They involve no sewing at all but do allow you to choose beautiful ribbon and pretty filigree tops. Again, they can be stored carefully for another year and you can have such fun adding to your collection each year.

1 Divide the fruit form into quarters by drawing lines on the polystyrene with a pen. Cover one quarter with gold sequins. Using gold pins, pin each sequin to the fruit form, cupped side down, making sure they overlap a little so that no polystyrene shows.

2 Cover alternate quarters with gold and silver sequins in the same way. The sequins need not overlap at the colour-joins, but they should butt up against one another.

3 Pin one end of the ribbon to the top of the fruit. Take the ribbon down to the bottom, so that it covers the join between the gold and silver sequins, pinning it in position with matching pins approximately every 2cm (³/₄in). Hold the ribbon in place with a pin pushed halfway in at the bottom.

4 Take the ribbon back up to the top, then turn it at a right-angle to wrap it over the remaining two joins and pin it in position. Bring the ribbon back down to the bottom again, take out the bottom pin and use it to secure both pieces of ribbon. Take the ribbon back up to the top, pin it in position and cut off any excess.

5 With the glass-headed pin, fix the filigree to the top of the fruit, covering the cut end of the ribbon.

CHAPTER FOUR

Formal
Dinner

Dinner parties are the most enormous fun to plan and hold. There is nothing nicer than being invited to someone's home for dinner when you know so much time, trouble and effort will have been put into the whole affair. Keeping a dinner party book is very useful, it will ensure that you don't repeat people or food combinations too often. The mix of people must be carefully thought out, as should the seating plan.

The menu should be such that, as a good hostess, you do not have to spend much time in the kitchen just before or during the party. Instead you can spend maximum time with your guests. This is vital from both your point of view and theirs; they have come to see you and you want to enjoy yourself as much as them, not feel that everybody else is having fun while you are slaving away in the kitchen – the fate of a flustered hostess.

Below: the ribbon bow on the name placements complements the ribbon used to tie the napkins.

Right: each place setting should be beautifully arranged and inviting.

Far right: simple to do yet so pretty to look at; a starter of smoked fish.

Planning the Table
and Food Presentation Ideas

If you use your dining only room for parties and at weekends, you can set your table two or three days before your dinner party. Apart from anything else, this spreads the effort involved in holding a dinner party, which is always an excellent idea. Choose a special tablecloth for the party; I adore white, for formality, and especially white-on-white embroidered linen or cotton, though damask is equally suitable. For added interest and glamour, laying something transparent and exquisite over your white cloth is sensational and adds an even greater touch of elegance to the table. Here we have used a fabulous double-layered white organdie fabric with wavy lines of black and white raffia inset between the two layers. Check, at least two days before, that you have the correct number of clean white, starched table napkins in the cupboard ready to be tied with ribbons. I often use an over-cloth and I love to tie napkins with pretty ribbons; depending on the fabrics and the formality of the ribbons, you can create very different looks, as you will see if you turn to the Christmas Lunch, (see page 30).

Setting the Table

Choose the best cutlery you have. For our menu a small knife and fork, a big knife and fork and a dessert spoon are needed. Lay the cutlery as you would use it moving from the outside in as you go through the courses. Ideally your table will be big enough for each person to have a side plate as well. Your glasses must sparkle and each person needs at least two – a tall, stemmed one for wine and a tumbler for water.

However, you may need more if you are having different wines with different courses. Always fill the water tumblers before seating everyone. Have wine coasters or mats to protect the tablecloth ready for the wine bottles (see page 44). With a hot starter, place the napkins on the table-mat, since you will not place the hot food there until after the guests have sat down. With a cold starter, place their napkins on the side plate, leaving the mat free for you to put the cold starter out before the guests arrive at the table. Light the candles just before they walk in.

Making name placements is such a fun, creative activity, apart from being the ultimate personal touch at the table – a way to make guests feel really special. Simple white, folded card looks excellent, but more decorative versions are even better (see page 46). Make them with removable name inserts so they can be reused often. Name placements are essential for three reasons: people can find where to sit without the host or hostess having to place them; they make guests feel special and wanted; if you have never met your dinner neighbour before, it is helpful to be able to remind yourself of their name by glancing at their placement.

- Table cloth, over-cloth, and napkins clean and all ironed.
- Lay the table up to three days in advance, as long as the room is not prone to dust.
- Plan seating arrangements and make name placements.
- Research and plan food presentation.

checklist

Presenting the Food

At a formal dinner, it is doubly nice if the food looks as attractive as the table, as well as tasting delicious. So spend some time thinking about the presentation. Food magazines and cookery books can be useful sources of inspiration, but don't pick ideas that are too complicated or you will be spending ages in the kitchen. A cold starter of pale pink smoked trout and stronger pink smoked salmon looks stunning. Lay out the fish in advance in a fan of alternate colours and cut stripes into the skin of a lemon with a sharp knife before you cut it into wedges. Keep the covered plates in the fridge, then add the lemon and horseradish at the last moment, just before you take the plates in.

A main course of glazed lamb chops, sautéed potatoes and vegetables can, with the exception of the vegetables, be done before the guests arrive. Marinade the lamb chops in honey, mustard and herbs, then bake them in a hot oven for thirty minutes. Once ready, they can be kept warm for an hour without spoiling. This goes for the sautéed potatoes as well, but cook the vegetables as close to serving as possible.

There are three alternative ways of presenting your main course. Plate up the food in the kitchen (no washing-up of serving dishes) and present each guest with a full plate. This is appropriate if you have no room for a sideboard in the dining room. The food will arrive very hot, but the two disadvantages are that the guests cannot personally select their food and you are kept away from the dining room for longer. If blessed with a sideboard, you can present the main course on a hotplate, in serving dishes. Or you can place the serving dishes on the table and pass them around. You need space on the table for this and a small oven glove, or napkin, to pass the hot dishes. For pudding I love to make tiramisù, as it can be made in a large entrée dish and is a favourite with almost everyone.

Strip of velvet measuring 17 x 44cm (6½ x 17¾in), plus a scrap for the bow

Ruler

Strip of interfacing measuring 6.75 x 41cm (2¾ x 16¼in)

Pins

44cm (17¾in) of 3.5cm- (1⅜in-) wide ribbon, plus 10cm (4in) for the bow

Matching sewing threads

Sewing machine

Circle of velvet measuring 16cm (6¼in) in diameter

Sewing needle

Circle of cork measuring 12.5cm (4⅞in) in diameter

Wine Coaster

One often sees silver wine coasters, but they can be expensive to buy and not always that easy to come by. Making one is very simple and you can have such fun selecting the perfect fabric to match your dining room and china. This velvet coaster, with its elegant tartan ribbon, looks very glamorous and some sort of stunning brocade would look equally good. It is best to make two, one for each end of the dining table.

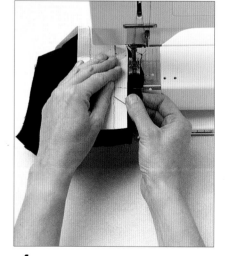

1 Measure and mark a line 8.5cm (3¼in) up from one long edge – across the middle of the strip of velvet – on the reverse.

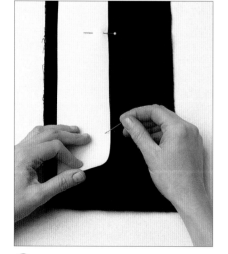

2 Pin the strip of interfacing to the back of the velvet, just below the marked line.

3 Pin the ribbon to the right side of the velvet, 3.5cm (1⅜in) up from the bottom. Pin through the velvet and the interfacing. Machine the ribbon in place, stitching close to the edges.

4 Right sides facing, stitch the short ends of the velvet together to form a tube. Then, right sides facing, pin the tube to the circle. Machine together through all the layers.

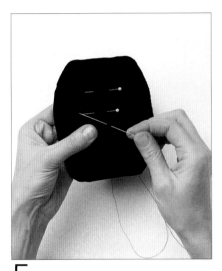

5 Fold the velvet down over the interfacing. Turn under the edge and pin, then stitch it to the edge of the circle. Turn right side out.

6 Make a bow from 10cm (4in) of ribbon, doubled, with a scrap of black velvet looped around the middle. Stitch the ends of the velvet together at the back.

7 Sew the centre back of the bow to the ribbon, on the front of the coaster. Anchor the corners of the bow to the top and bottom of the ribbon with tiny stab stitches.

8 Slip the circle of cork into the bottom of the coaster.

materials

Rectangle of card measuring 10 x 11cm (4 x 4½in)

Ruler

Scissors

Cutting mat

Craft knife

Hole puncher

30cm (12in) length of 2mm- (⅛in-) wide ribbon

Strip of card measuring 1.9 x 10.5cm (¹¹⁄₁₆ x 4¼in)

Italic pen

Name Placements

These are so simple to make yet look fantastic on the dinner table, giving it that indisputably glamorous finishing touch. You could design anything you like, but I feel these four designs are particularly special. Making them changeable, so that you can use them for the next dinner party is ingenious. It is definitely worth buying an italic pen to write with, or a white pen if you are using black card – and asking someone with lovely handwriting to write them for you.

Changeable Placement with Ribbon

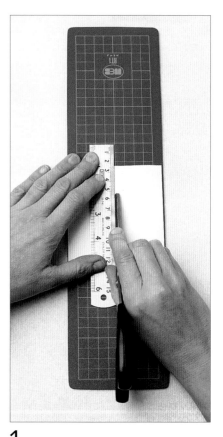

1 Mark the halfway point across the 10cm (4in) width of the rectangle of card with tiny pencil dots. With a metal ruler and the back of the blade of closed scissors, score a line across the card at the marked point. Work on a cutting mat to protect your worksurface. Fold the card in half on the scored line.

2 Fold the card out flat again. On the front, measure and mark 1.5cm (⅝in) in from each end and 1.5cm (⅝in) down from the top and up from the bottom. With a metal ruler and a craft knife, cut a 2cm (¾in) slot in the card between the marked points, ensuring that you cut cleanly right up to the marks.

3 Punch a hole in the top left-hand corner of the front of the card, making sure that it does not touch the cut slot.

4 Tie the ribbon in a bow through the hole. To tie the perfect bow, thread the ribbon through the hole, then take the end of the ribbon in your left hand over the end in your right hand. Bring this end up through the loop to form a single knot. Make a small loop with the ribbon now in your left hand; this loop should point to the right. Take the ribbon in your right hand down over and round the loop and tie a bow. Pull the bow tight then adjust the ends

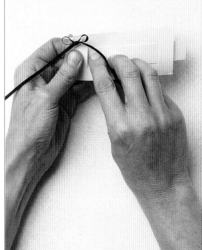

5 Tuck one end of the narrow strip of card into one of the slots and the other end into the other slot. When you are ready to write the guest's names, slip this strip of card out of the slots, write the name on it and slip it back in again. To change the name, just change the narrow strip of card.

Rectangle of card measuring 10 x 11cm (4 x 4½in)

Ruler

Scissors

Cutting mat

Craft knife

15cm (6in) of 2mm- (⅛in-) wide ribbon

Needle with wide eye

White pen

Placement with Woven Ribbon

This placement can be made either as a simple folded rectangle of card as shown here, or as a changeable one as shown before.

1 Score and fold the card as before. Cut a row of 3mm- (¼in-) wide vertical slots 1cm (½in) above the bottom of the front of the placement. You must have an even number of slots so that both ends of the woven ribbon will show at the front.

2 Thread the needle with the ribbon and, starting from the front, weave it in and out of the slots. If the ribbon twists, pull the end to draw it through the slots to untwist it and then pull it back again. Trim the ends of the ribbon at an angle.

Placement with Bow

The bow used on this placement can simply be pulled off and glued on to a new one when you need to change the name.

1 Score and fold the card as before. Dab a spot of glue on the centre of the front of the placement, right at the top. Stick the bow in place so that when the card is folded the loops stand up above the top edge.

materials

Rectangle of card measuring 10 x 11cm (4 x 4½in)

Ruler

Scissors

Cutting mat

PVA glue

Small ready-made bow from haberdashery shop, or a hand-tied bow

Italic pen

Placement with Ribbon Frame

1 Score and fold the larger piece of card as before. Lay the ribbon against each side of the front of the placement in turn, marking off the length with pins.

2 Cut the ribbon at each pin to give two long and two short pieces. Using the fine paintbrush, glue the long pieces to the top and bottom of the front of the placement.

materials

Rectangle of card measuring 10 x 11cm (4 x 4½in)

Ruler

Scissors

Cutting mat

32cm (13in) of 1.5cm- (⅝in-) wide ribbon

Pins

PVA glue

Fine paintbrush

Craft knife

Rectangle of card measuring 9 x 10cm (3½ x 4in)

Sticky putty

White pen

3 Insert a pin 1.5cm (⅝in) from each end of each short piece of ribbon, then cut a 45° diagonal from the pin to the end of the ribbon. Glue the short pieces to the sides of the placement. The diagonal ends give a mitred effect.

4 Cut out the centre of the card to make a frame. Work on a cutting mat and with a craft knife start cutting each side from one end, then, just before you get to the other end, change direction and cut from that end to get a perfect corner. Stick the smaller rectangle of card to the back of the ribbon frame with sticky putty or a tiny dab of glue and write the guest's name on it. To change the name, just change this piece of card.

CHAPTER FIVE

Outdoor Lunch

Any excuse to eat outside is welcome – the food always seems to taste better. It also offers a perfect opportunity to indulge yourself in a lot of colour, in both food and tableware, especially if lunch is to be set out on a wooden table. You don't want to start covering outdoor tables with cloths, as this starts to defeat the object of eating outside, which should be informal and done with the minimum of fuss.

The food should go out at the last moment, since the sun can easily spoil it, and be kept covered for as long as possible. In case the weather lets you down, make sure it's the sort of lunch that can easily be reversed into the house; food for a barbecue can be successfully grilled or roasted in the oven if necessary. Of course, it can still be cooked in the rain: the food won't mind – just check that the chef doesn't and then give them an umbrella.

Planning to Eat Outdoors

If you happen to have a shed near your outdoor lunch venue, you can leave things in there, throughout the summer, that you use every time you eat outside. I have four identical jars, with pretty lids, all in one small basket. These jars hold instant coffee, ordinary teabags, herbal teabags and sugar. I also have a practical metal holder full of paper napkins, which makes them easy to store and give out. Big, wide baskets are the best way of transporting food to the outdoor table, rather than trays that require two hands and are limited in capacity.

Watching the Weather

If there is a possibility of it being really hot during lunch, make sure you can create some shade. While some of us love to get a suntan and will soak up as much heat as possible, there are masses of people who don't like the sun and feel very uncomfortable in it. Have a selection of hats in a large basket for both adults and children (who are often unaware that they are getting sunburnt). Baseball caps are the easiest to store. Pull the table partially under a tree – this means you can keep both the sun worshippers and the shade lovers happy. If there are no trees around, you could consider buying a canopy or large umbrella; or you might construct a basic timber structure or put up tent poles and cover them with fabric.

Have spare coats, fleeces and sweatshirts handy for those less-hot summer days. It is very hard to enjoy an outdoor lunch when you are blue with cold. Perhaps include hot soup in your menu to warm people up. If you don't need it in the end, you can always have it later at dinner, or freeze it. If it starts to rain, just whisk everything inside and lay it all out quickly in the kitchen.

Children

Don't expect small children to sit still for long; they don't have the same interest in food and chat as an adult. Let them leave the table after the main course so they can have a lovely time playing in the garden until it's time for pudding. Once they have finished eating, ask each child to make just one journey into the kitchen with a full basket or tray: this will make the clearing-up much easier. Make sure smaller children carry only plastic, metal, basketware or wood, so that no harm can come to them or anything else if things are accidentally dropped. In terms of seating, if you run out of space at the table, children are usually happy on rugs on the grass.

Setting the Table

You don't need flowers on the table when you are eating outdoors. However, little pots of herbs look good and smell sweet. Complement your colourful tableware with pretty fabric bread baskets (see page 56). They can be made in almost any size and can be absolutely stuffed with bread rolls and still look attractive.

A jug cover not only looks pretty (see page 58), especially if you work a beaded or embroidered design on it, but also serves such a useful purpose: you can put out your jugs of drink before lunch, knowing no unwelcome creature will gain access.

Left: look out for stylish accessories, like these straws with their paper lemons.

Below left and centre: kebabs, either vegetable or meat, are both tasty and easy to prepare and cook.

Below right: this clever contraption holds paper napkins securely and accessibly.

- Weather forecast.
- Hats for sun and spare clothes for cool weather.
- Baskets to carry everything outside in.
- Colourful and sturdy crockery and glassware.
- Food that is easy to cook and eat and that can be cooked in the kitchen if necessary
- Enough comfortable seating for all guests, including rugs for children to sit on.

checklist

Summer Salads

Sunny days and outdoor eating automatically make you think of salads. These offer an unrivalled opportunity to combine colour, texture and taste in dozens of marvellous ways. You can include many ingredients: just think of things that you like and put them together. On these pages are a few of my favourite combinations.

Undressed salads are so dull. I love a piquant dressing with both English and grainy mustard, cider vinegar, honey, salt, pepper and very good olive oil (you can also add garlic to this if you wish). I make this dressing by putting all the ingredients except the oil into a food processor and then dripping in the oil while the processor is running. This will produce a dressing that is pale and creamy and never separates. However, it may prove to be too thick, so dilute it to a pouring consistency by adding a few tablespoons of boiling water. Add the dressing to the salad just before you serve it.

Above: transform an ordinary green salad into a colourful feast for the eyes by adding edible nasturtium flowers. Make up and dress the salad as usual then lay the flowers on top just before serving it.

Above: this rich tomato barbecue sauce is made in exactly the same way as the sauce for tomato croutes (see page 108 for recipe). However, to give it an extra barbecue tang, add balsamic vinegar and brown sugar to taste. It also makes a tempting dip for crusty Italian bread.

Above: another vibrant salad that also has loads of texture. Peel and grate carrots then combine them with currants (for a sweet element), sesame seeds and coriander, for colour. Dress the salad with a little sesame oil.

Left: (far left) baby plum tomatoes, luscious black olives, cubes of feta cheese and fresh basil leaves make up a salad as striking as it is delicious. (Left) a simple mix of tender young spinach leaves and crispy croutons offsets the stronger flavours perfectly.

Fabric Bread Basket

This is the easiest thing in the world to make. It is washable and stores away easily, unlike baskets, which are fairly clumsy things to store and tend to gather dust. If you had a large lunch party outside, it would look so pretty to have lots of these all along the table. The beads are exactly the tiny, eye-catching detail that I love.

materials

Two squares of fabric measuring 50cm (20in) square

Pins

Sewing machine

Matching sewing thread

Iron

Sewing needle

Strip of fabric measuring 8 x 16cm (3 x 6¼in)

Beading needle

4 small beads

1 Right sides facing, pin and machine the fabric squares together, leaving a small gap on one side.

**2** Turn the square right side out and press, then slip stitch the gap closed.

3 Press under 1.5cm (5/8in) on each side of the strip of fabric, then press it in half and topstitch close to the open edge.

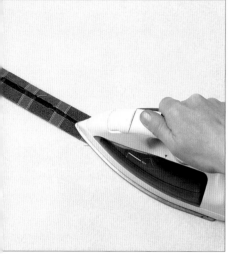

4 Thread the beading needle and secure the thread at the back of one corner of the fabric. Take it through the corner, through a bead and back through the fabric. Fold the strip in half and take the needle through both ends of it, then through the opposite corner of the square of fabric.

5 Take the needle through another bead. Go back and forth through all the layers of fabric and both beads several times, then secure the thread.

6 Draw up the remaining corners and stitch them together, with beads, as described in steps 4 and 5.

materials

Circle of fabric large enough in diameter to cover the mouth of your jug, plus 10cm (4in)

Pins

Matching sewing thread

Sewing needle

Iron

Beading needle

Beading thread

25g (1oz) bugle beads

25 leaf-shaped beads

Beaded Jug Cover

This is both pretty and practical, as it stops flies making mischief in your cool summer drinks. The glass leaves we used are so suitable, as they add weight to hold the cover in place. This project may look complicated, but once you have got the hang of couched beading, it is simple, though it does take a little time. Alternatively, you can sew on lengths of narrow satin ribbon instead of lines of beads and loop it through heavier beads at the edges.

1 Slip stitch a narrow double hem all around the fabric circle. Press the circle in half, then in half the other way to make clear creases.

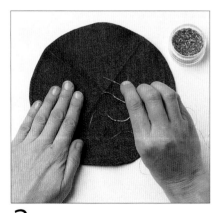

2 Thread the beading needle and bring it up through the centre of the fabric circle. Thread on enough beads to reach the edge of the circle. Push the needle into the fabric to keep it out of the way, but leave it threaded.

3 Thread the sewing needle and bring it up through the fabric, on a crease line, approximately 1cm (1/2in) from the centre. Lay the line of beads down along the crease, then take the second thread over the beads and back down through the fabric to couch the beads in position.

4 On the reverse of the fabric, take the thread along the crease approximately 1cm (1/2in), then bring it back through to the front. Take another stitch over the line of beads. Repeat this process right along the crease. At the edge of the fabric, on the reverse, weave the thread through the line of stitches back to the centre, then set it aside.

5 Pick up the beading needle with the beads threaded on and thread on fifteen more beads. Then thread on a leaf bead, then three more beads. Take the needle back through the fourth bead up from the leaf and through all the other beads right back up to the edge of the fabric.

6 Pull the tail up fairly tight. Thread the needle back through all the beads in the couched line, then make a tiny stitch in the centre to secure it. Couch a line of beads along each of the four creases and make a tail with a leaf at the end of each one. Couch four more lines, with tails and leaves, between these, giving eight lines in total.

7 Bead the edge of the jug cover by making tiny running stitches, with a bead threaded on to every stitch, right around the very edge.

8 Add two more leaves between each couched line. For each leaf, take a stitch through the edge of the fabric, thread on three beads, then a leaf, then three more beads. Take the needle back through the fabric and secure the thread.

9 In the same way, add a single leaf to the centre of the jug cover, where the lines of beading meet.

House Guests

Having friends come to stay with you, whether it is just for a night or for a few days, is such brilliant fun. You can spend some time just catching up on each other's news and gossip and you can also plan events or trips that you will all enjoy. In fact, planning is one of the most important elements of entertaining house guests.

In this chapter we deal with three very different types of house guests: a midweek overnight guest; teenage girls at a sleepover party; and a weekend guest. With a midweek guest the most important thing is that you fit them smoothly into your routine so that they do not feel they are imposing and that you, and your family, do not find the visit stressful.

Teenage girls will be oblivious of many of the details that an adult guest would notice, but they do need to be kept occupied and happy, so we have chosen favourite simple recipes and easy projects to make. On the other hand, a weekend guest needs quite a lot of attention paid to their room, as it will be their home for a few days. For this guest we have given lots of ideas to make them welcome.

Midweek Overnight Guest

A midweek overnight guest is often self-invited (the most flattering thing in the world), as you would generally choose to entertain at the weekend, as opposed to weekdays when motherhood and work are top priorities. But with good planning your guest can fit into your life with ease. Get everything ready before the children return from school, so that help with homework is not diluted by anxious attention to cooking, the guest bedroom and table laying. All three courses of dinner should either be prepared earlier or be ones you can cook moments before serving. Your guest is bound to want a bath or some quiet time before supper – a chance for you to quietly lay the table now that the children's tea and homework are over.

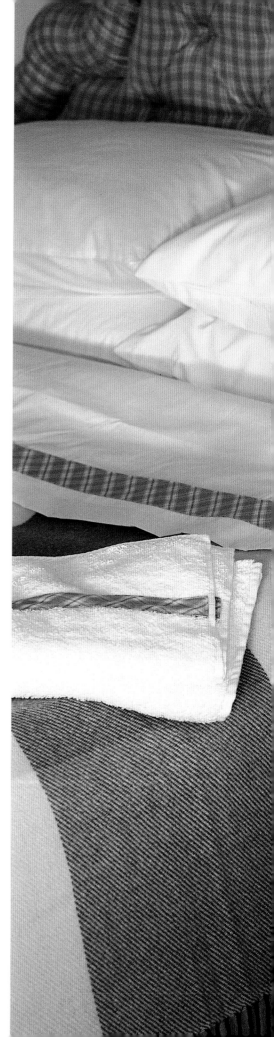

**BUTTERNUT AND
SWEET POTATO SOUP**
Chop an onion and sweat it
slowly, so that it does not
brown, in a little olive oil. Once
transparent, add a peeled and
chopped butternut squash, and
a sweet potato. Pour in 300ml
(½ pint, 1¼ cups) of vegetable
stock. Simmer until the
vegetables are totally soft.
Liquidize the soup then return
it to the pan and add 300ml
(½ pint, 1¼ cups) of milk and
seasoning. Reheat without
allowing the soup to boil.

Planning Ahead
and Quick Food

You really need to shop for and prepare your guest's supper, breakfast and flowers the
day before they arrive. To do all this on the same day, on top of caring for the children
and meeting work deadlines, would be all too much to fit into an already full day. It is
inevitable that the telephone will ring – or there might even be an unforeseen minor
drama with your children. While dealing with all of this it's reassuring to know, at the
back of your mind, that everything is basically ready.

Preparing the Bedroom

The bedroom can also be done in advance. It is easy to trim a towel to match the furnishings in the guest room (see
page 66) and, for an extra special touch, to make matching covered coat hangers for the room (see page 68).
Obviously, these are projects to make in your own time, not the night before your guest comes to stay! The linen must
be perfect and always provide a folded hand towel and lovely big bath towel – they are so luxurious. If you keep the
linen for each room labelled and categorized (see page 84), then it is easy to find the correct pile in the cupboard.

Fresh flowers are a loving touch that I do think is worth the small effort involved, as they carry such a special
message. It doesn't have to be a big display; a small bunch of sweet-smelling freesias or narcissi is perfect. Keep a
small vase in the room so that you don't have to go hunting for one every time guests come to stay.

A really useful thing for your guest is a little sewing kit in their room. Again, you can make one to match the
furnishings (see page 70). Keep a drawer supplied with spare toiletries such as cotton wool, bath essences and soap,

and then you can quickly replenish any depleted stocks in the guest bedroom. Tired after a long day, your visitor will really appreciate a little pampering.

Once your children's tea is over, lay the table with candles and napkins. Take the relevant dishes out of the fridge, ready to warm up or bake. When the children are settled or in bed, you can sit down with your friend to enjoy each other's company and catch up on news.

Planning the Food

The menu needs careful thought so that all the elements can feasibly be made within your usual schedule. One of my favourite menus is butternut and sweet potato soup with croutons and parsley, followed by prawns on a bed of sautéed leeks, which are then baked in the oven with crème fraiche and parmesan. For pudding I suggest rhubarb fool made with Greek yoghurt and stem ginger and served with ginger shortbread.

The soup can be made days before, as it freezes superbly. Croutons add a special touch to soup and can also be made in advance from any bread then stored in an airtight container. The prawn dish can be put together the day before, but not baked; all you need to do on the night is pop it in the oven. I make rhubarb purée in batches and store it in jars or bags in the freezer. Simply unfreeze it the day before and combine it with the yoghurt and finely chopped stem ginger. The shortbread will also live blissfully in the freezer; just place it in a warm oven to crisp it up before serving it. As you can see, with this menu you spend the minimum of time in the kitchen and the maximum with your friend.

- Shopping, cooking and cleaning.
- Table setting, flowers and napkins.
- Linen and hot-water bottles or an electric blanket if it is cold.
- Towels and bath mat.
- Soap, bath essences and talcum powder.
- Tooth mug, tissues and cotton wool.
- Light bulbs, wastepaper bin and coat hangers.

checklist

materials

5cm- (2in-) wide strip of fabric, cut on the cross, the length of which measures 2cm (¾in) longer than the width of the towel

Ruler

Scissors

Iron

Pins

Towel

Matching sewing thread

Sewing machine

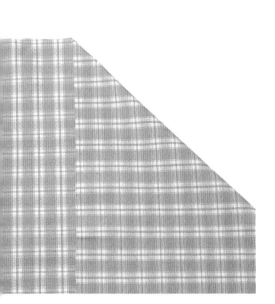

1 Fold one edge of the fabric over at 90° to establish a diagonal. The fabric we used is checked, so in fact we folded it at an angle just under 90° so that the diagonal line ran neatly through the pattern.

Trimmed Towel

This really does look extremely special as you walk into the room. It is so quick and easy to make that it is lovely to take the idea a step further and trim a flannel and sheet to match. You don't have to cut the fabric on the cross but, with checks, it does give the item even more style.

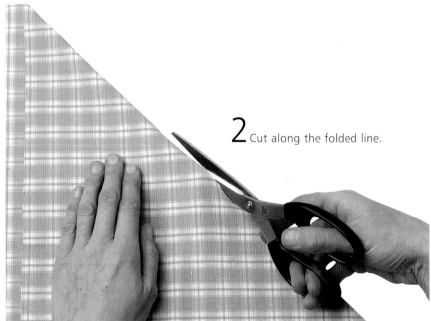

2 Cut along the folded line.

3 Measure 5cm (2in) from the cut edge and cut a strip of fabric. If your towel has a flat, braided strip across it, check the width of that and cut the fabric 2.5cm (1in) wider.

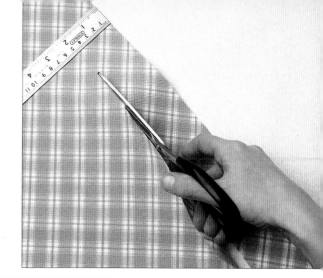

4 Press under 1cm (½in) on all sides of the strip.

5 Pin the strip across the end of the towel. If your towel is plain, pin the strip approximately 12cm (4¾in) up from the edge. If it has a flat strip, pin the fabric over that.

6 Machine the strip to the towel along all four sides, topstitching close to the edges.

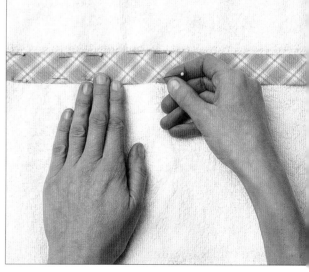

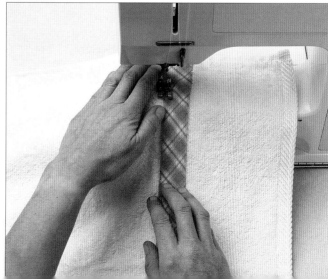

materials

- **Wooden coat hanger**
- **Strip of interlining measuring 12 x 50cm (4³⁄₄ x by 20in)**
- **Pins**
- **Polyester sewing thread**
- **Sewing needle**
- **Scissors**
- **Strip of fabric measuring 12 x 90cm (4³⁄₄ x 35in)**
- **Iron**
- **Sewing machine**
- **Ribbon for bow**

Covered **Coat Hanger**

Few things are more dispiriting for a visitor than discovering that there is no hanging space at all, or not nearly enough coat hangers, or only metal hangers. By contrast, imagine how lovely it is for your guest to open the cupboard door and find a neat row of pretty coat hangers, which match other soft furnishings in the room. These are easy to make in your lap and are maintenance-free because they remain looking gorgeous for years. As well as looking inviting, these hangers will also help to keep clothes in mint condition.

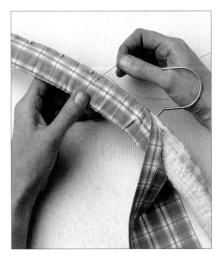

2 Press under 2cm (³⁄₄in) along each long edge of the fabric. Then, fold it in half widthways and machine up the two short ends.

1 Fold the strip of interlining in half around the coat hanger. Tuck in the ends and stitch up the sides and along the top using backstitch. Trim off the excess interlining along the top of the coat hanger.

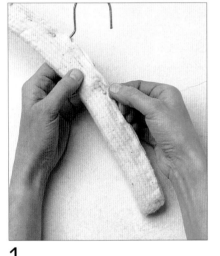

3 Fold the fabric in half lengthways and cut a notch in the middle.

4 With the notch lined up with the hook of the coat hanger, fold the fabric over the interlining and stitch the edges together, on one side of the hook, using a small running stitch. Stitch up a short section at a time.

5 With your fingers, ruche the stitched fabric up along the coat hanger towards the hook. Stitch another section and ruche it up, continuing until you are 5cm (2in) from the end of the fabric. With your thumb and index finger, roll the pressed-under edge of the fabric a little deeper so that it sits tightly round the end of the hanger. Stitch up the last section. If you find that the fabric slips off a little at the ends, a discreet vertical staple at the end of the hanger, between the ruching, will hold it in place. Tie a piece of toning ribbon in a bow around the base of the hook.

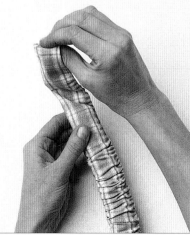

**Rectangle of main fabric
measuring 12 x 19cm
(4³/₄ x 7¹/₂in)**

Iron

**Rectangle of fusible webbing
measuring 10 x 17cm
(3³/₄ x 6¹/₂in)**

**8cm (3in) length of 2mm-
(¹/₈in-) wide ribbon**

Matching sewing thread

Sewing needle

Button

**Two pinked rectangles
of felt measuring 9 x 16cm
(3¹/₂ x 6¹/₄in)**

**Skein of six-stranded
embroidery thread**

Embroidery needle

Sewing Kit

This is not only a really sweet thing to put on your guest's dressing table, but it would also make a gorgeous Christmas or birthday present to a dear friend. It is something a child could make with enormous ease and get such a sense of achievement from once it is done. It is so tiny and useful that you might consider making one to live permanently in your luggage.

1 Turn under and press 1cm (¹/₂in) all round the rectangle of main fabric. Mitre the corners by pressing over a triangle at the point where the pressed lines meet at each corner. Then refold the corners and press them flat.

2 Lay the rectangle of fusible webbing into the centre section of the main fabric, tucking it under the pressed-under edges. Iron it in place.

3 Fold the length of ribbon in half and stitch the raw ends to the centre of the pressed-under edge of one short side of the main fabric. The looped end of the ribbon will protrude beyond the edge of the fabric.

4 Stitch a button to the other short edge of the front of the main fabric, in a corresponding position to the ribbon loop.

5 Peel the paper backing off the fusible webbing. Lay one of the rectangles of felt centrally on top of the fusible webbing. The pinked edges should sit over the pressed-under edges of the fabric, with an equal amount showing all round. Iron the felt in place, bonding it to the webbing.

6 Using three strands of embroidery thread, work a line of running stitch right round the edge of the main fabric, stitching through the fabric and the felt to hold the edges in place. Don't worry if the stitches are not perfectly even; the hand-stitched look adds to the sewing kit's charm.

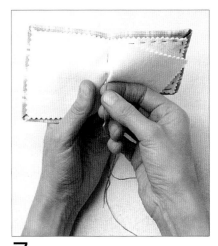

7 Fold the sewing kit and the remaining rectangle of felt in half and press them. Centre the felt on the kit, aligning the pressed folds. Using strands of embroidery thread, stitch the two fabrics together, through all the layers, with running stitch. Put needles and pins into the felt pages and pin in looped lengths of thread.

CHAPTER SEVEN

Sleepover Party

Girls will love the novelty of being creative with cooking, painting or sewing instead of playing computer games or watching videos. They will get such a lovely sense of achievement when they have made something themselves, especially something that has instantly pleasing uses, such as a little terracotta pot to store their bathroom paraphernalia in.

It is even better when their efforts have a means to an end: delicious cooking that both satisfies the girls' hunger and produces food for a midnight feast is always popular. Let them choose their favourite goodies from a selection of easy recipes.

Quite apart from being huge fun and keeping the girls occupied for ages, all of these activities involve both learning new skills and developing a basic training – both of which will be so useful in later life.

Planning
a Sleepover

Young girls love a sleepover and, as a mother, there is no need for you to dread it in terms of chaos and disruption in your house. However, it is worth just investing a little bit of time and thought in the planning of the event so that it will all run smoothly.

Preparing the Bedroom

One of the most important things is to ensure that everyone is going to be happy all the time, with no one feeling left out – so the sleeping arrangements are important. It is best to let all the girls share one room; most teenagers are so relaxed when it comes to sleeping that they seem to be able to sleep anywhere. You may have a twin-bedded room with enough space for more than two to sleep. There are various alternatives for extra beds: camp beds, Z-beds, an inflatable mattress, or a mattress borrowed from another bedroom. The girls will often just curl up on the floor in a nest of duvets and all fall asleep in a great big huddle when the chatting finally peters out. If you are short of bedding, ask the girls to bring their own sleeping bags, though it is easier all round if you can provide a pillow and towel.

Entertaining the Girls

Children love being occupied with a variety of activities as well as 'veging out' and just chatting. Most enjoy cooking and painting and will find that decorating a flowerpot brings out the artist in them (see page 80). Keep the pots in the bathroom so that all the tooth and hair accessories can be tidied away in them and not lost or muddled up. Encourage the girls to paint a design to match the motif on their laundry bag (see page 78), so it will be easy for everyone to know whose pot and bag is whose. The laundry bag could always return with the child whenever she

- Enough beds made up.
- Recipes for favourite biscuits written out and ingredients all assembled.
- Pots, paints and paintbrushes ready.
- Laundry bags washed.
- Breakfast planned.

checklist

Above left: if the girls are artistically inclined, ask them to paint their own pots. If not, paint them yourself; you'll have fun.

Above: take any breakables out of the bedroom before the girls arrive, then let them go a little wild. An enthusiastic pillow fight is just the best fun.

comes to stay (assuming she is a regular visitor), or you can wash them and keep them in the linen cupboard for the next sleepover. These bags are really useful, for both the child and her mother, who will inevitably have to sort out and wash the clothes later.

Always let the girls sleep in for ages in the morning; it is a great treat and they will have lost out on sleep by talking for half the night. Also, the bedroom is a marvellous place for discussing all those vital things, such as what to wear and what make-up and accessories to use, so give them as much privacy as possible.

Planning the Food

Make supper a fairly simple one that, with luck, appeals to all. Most youngsters love pasta with interesting sauces and garlic bread. Always offer pudding; vanilla ice cream is fine, with delicious chocolate or butterscotch sauce that takes only minutes to make. Put candles on the table to make the evening feel special. Breakfast can be a totally movable feast. Crispy bacon usually goes down a treat and the girls can eat it with their fingers when they surface from the bedroom. Croissants, pain au chocolat and Danish pastries are deeply delicious for breakfast, together with cereals.

Children always leave something behind, so check under beds, in the garden and all around the house before they go.

SHORTBREAD

Put 50g (2oz, ¼ cup) of butter and 100g (4oz, ½ cup) of sugar in a food processor and blend. Add 150g (6oz, 1½ cups) of plain flour and 2 tsp of ground cinnamon. Process, with a sharp blade, until the mixture starts to look like damp dough. Heavily butter a tin and press the mixture into it. Bake at 150°C/300°F/gas mark 2 for 30min. Cut into squares while still hot and allow to cool before lifting out of the tin.

CHOCOLATE BROWNIES

Melt 350g (12oz, 1½ cups) of margarine in a large saucepan with 175g (6oz, 6 squares) of chocolate. Add 25g (1oz, ¼ cup) of cocoa powder and 25g (1oz, ¼ cup) of drinking-chocolate powder. Whisk 5 eggs with 550g (20oz, 2¼ cups) of granulated sugar together in a food processor. Add a few drops of vanilla essence. Pour all this into the chocolate mixture. Stir in the walnuts. Butter a large roasting tin and pour in the mixture. Bake at 190°C/375°F/gas mark 5 for 30min. Do not overcook the brownies as they are so good when very soft. Served with thick cream, these are easily good enough for a dinner-party pudding.

Making Biscuits

Simple cooking is a really good way of keeping children occupied, though you should be close by to supervise them. They gossip, eat the ingredients and are bound to get distracted and burn one of their efforts. However, they thoroughly enjoy themselves, all the more so because later they get to eat the delicious things that they have made,

and there is nothing quite so fulfilling (or in this case, just filling), as enjoying the fruits of ones own labours. Write out the simple recipes, get all the ingredients together for them and then just take a back seat while they cook.

I tend to make biscuits in large batches as I know from experience that sweet, sticky things are very tempting. It is so good to have a tin full of goodies in the kitchen, ready to be offered to whoever drops in for lunch or tea. All these biscuits freeze beautifully; it's worth freezing them, as they stay a lot fresher and they are so quick to unfreeze.

FLAPJACKS

Melt 100g (4oz, 1/2 cup) butter (don't use margarine, as it really doesn't work) and 1 tbsp of syrup in a large pan. Stir in 75g (3oz, 3/4 cup) of cornflakes or crisped-rice breakfast cereal, 50g (2oz, 1/2 cup) of flaked oats, 50g (2oz, 1/2 cup) of self-raising flour and 100g (4oz, 1/2 cup) of caster sugar. Butter a baking tray and pour the mixture in, bearing in mind that it will rise a little. Bake at 200°C/400°F/ gas mark 6 for 15min. Cut the flapjack into squares while it is still hot and allow them to cool before lifting out of the tin.

materials

Square of fabric for the motif square measuring 14cm (5½in) square

Iron

Dressmaker's carbon paper

Pencil

Bird template on page 125

Cream sewing thread

Sewing machine

Pins

Rectangle of main fabric measuring 100 x 65cm (39 x 26in)

Ruler

Matching sewing thread

150cm (59in) of cord

PVA glue

Below: a simple heart is another pretty motif for a laundry page. The template is given on page 125.

Laundry Bag

These are very quick sewing projects and serve such a practical purpose once done. The little motif is fun and ties in with the flowerpot, but it is not essential if you are in a real hurry. If you cannot get the right colour cord, any type of ribbon or tape would do the trick. Never make these too small; it's amazing how much space a dirty sweatshirt, pair of jeans and a T-shirt take up.

1 Press under 1cm (½in) all round the square of motif fabric. Enlarge the template to the required size and transfer the outline on to the fabric with dressmaker's carbon paper.

2 Machine-embroider the motif onto the fabric. Your sewing-machine manual should give the setting for machine embroidery, but always practise on a scrap of the same fabric first.

3 Using a small zigzag stitch, stitch the motif square on to the main fabric. It should be 5cm (2in) up from the bottom edge and 35cm (14in) from one side edge.

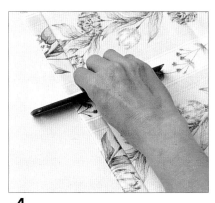

4 Using a small metal ruler, measure and scrape a 1.5cm (5/8in) hem, then a 2cm (3/4in) hem across one long side of the main fabric.

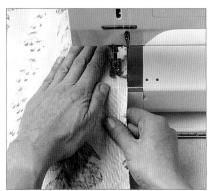

5 Unfold the scraped hem. Right sides facing, fold the fabric in half and machine across the bottom and up the side to within 3cm (1¼in) of the top pressed edge.

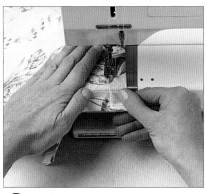

6 On the last 3cm (1¼in) of the side of the bag, fold the raw edges to the wrong side and refold the scraped hem over them. Machine round the top, close to the pressed edge, to make a channel for the cord.

7 Thread the cord through the channel and tie the ends together in a knot. Dab a little PVA glue on the ends of the cord to prevent it from fraying.

Terracotta flowerpot

Thick and thin paintbrushes

Pink and blue acrylic paint

Bird template on page 125

Carbon paper

Pencil

Painted Storage Pot

Children can discover hidden talents with this project. They could paint straight onto the pot, but giving the motif a pretty background colour increases the appeal. If the motif can tie in with the embroidery on the laundry bag, so much the better. A painted terracotta pot filled with hyacinths is a really sweet present for a child to give at Christmas.

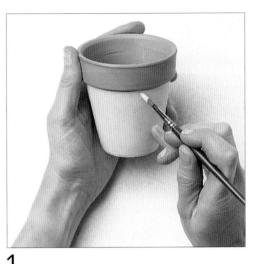

1 Using the thicker paintbrush, paint the main part of the pot with two coats of pink paint. Leave it to dry.

2 Enlarge the template to the right size and use a piece of carbon paper to transfer the design on to the pot. Paint over the carbon lines with blue paint, using the thin paintbrush. You can also add stripes or spots to the unpainted rim of the pot. You can varnish the finished pot, once it is dry, to seal your work.

Weekend
Guests

It is lovely to be able to offer your weekend guests an immaculate bedroom – full of all the essential comforts designed to make their stay perfect. On a long-term basis, I tend to protect furnishings in the guest bedroom, to a certain extent, so that they always look bright and fresh. This can be done either by keeping the roller blinds (window shades) down, in between guests staying, or by using dustsheets or throw-over loose covers on the furnishings.

If your guests arrive late on Friday evening, having fought the traffic and possibly worried about finding you, they deserve a particularly special welcome. Therefore they should walk into a warm bedroom, where the lights are on, the curtains drawn and the bed turned down. If they arrive before dusk, find a moment during the evening to go into the room and do these simple things.

Left: put a tiny posy of flowers on the bedside table, even if you place a larger arrangement elsewhere in the room.

Below: pretty linen makes all the difference in a guest bedroom, so do make sure that it is ironed and looks its best.

Planning
for Guests

Planning a weekend with friends to stay is always huge fun, but it does require thinking through first from a social, culinary and comfort point of view. If you are going to invite a family, do their children get on with yours? Will your children be too much for a person who is not used to having them around? Work all this out, then pick up the telephone. Prepare the room on Wednesday (with a final check on Friday), the food on Thursday and the flowers on Friday. This way the effort is evenly spread.

Storing Linen

Keep the guest linen on a shelf in the airing cupboard. If the bedroom is blue, have the shelf labelled 'Blue Room' or tie a piece of blue ribbon around it. Colour-code both ends of each piece of linen with a tiny, doubled-over, machined-on loop of matching ribbon. This makes it easy to return the linen to the right shelf after washing so that it is there whenever you need it.

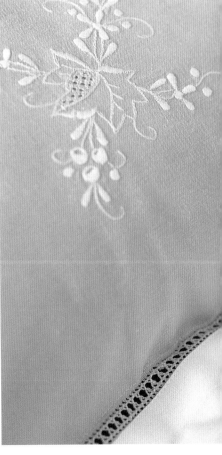

Right: I love a fruit salad for breakfast, but half a grapefruit, with just a little brown sugar sprinkled on top, is a lovely alternative.

Left: check in advance whether your guests prefer tea or coffee in the morning, as it really does make a difference to most people. A glass of fresh orange juice is good for those who prefer to avoid caffeine.

Preparing the Room

A guest for two days needs to unpack, so check the drawers; there should be a lavender bag (see page 86) in each and no items left by a previous guest. The cupboard should be empty apart from spare blankets and coat hangers. Check there are books, writing paper and a comfortable chair. Never do the flowers before Friday, or they may droop by Sunday.

Make the bed, put out the towels and sewing kit. Spray the pillows with linen spray and check that all the essential toiletries like tissues, cleansing pads, soap, etc are fresh and ready. Check the heating and hot water and pop a hot-water bottle (see page 87) between the sheets if the weather is cold, just before your guest arrives. With all this behind you, you will feel totally relaxed on the evening they arrive.

The Perfect Breakfast

Have the tray all laid out the night before, with everything ready in the fridge to add to the tray the next morning. Leave the little butter dish out of the fridge so that the butter will be soft. Offer delicious pastries, such as croissants or pain au chocolat, with fresh fruit for a lighter note. Make the tray look attractive and, if possible, offer a newspaper or favourite magazine to complete the treat.

- Maps or clear directions sent to first-time visitors.
- Linen for guest room washed and all stored on the right shelf.
- Room, food and flowers prepared.
- Books and writing paper in the room.
- Breakfast tray planned and linen washed.

checklist

Lavender Bag

These are such a treat and the sign of a really good, caring hostess. The wonderful aroma of lavender that wafts out of the drawers is so soothing for your guests. You will probably have to replace the bags every other year as lavender looses its scent, but they are so quick to make that you won't mind doing this.

materials

Two squares of organza, each measuring 15cm (6in) square

Pins

Ruler

Blue thread

Sewing machine

Piece of paper (a sheet of writing paper is ideal)

Dried lavender

Pinking shears

1 Pin the squares of organza together. Set the machine to a narrow satin stitch and using blue thread, machine a square 3cm (1¼in) in from the edges of the organza. Leave a small gap in one side.

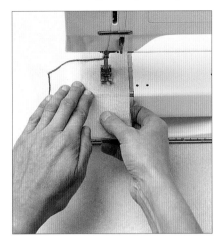

2 Roll a piece of paper into a funnel and slide the narrow end into the gap in the satin stitching. Pour dried lavender down the funnel into the organza bag. Fill the bag until it is quite plump. Pin, then machine the gap closed.

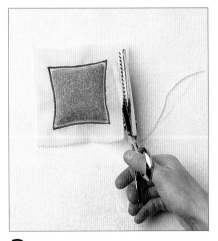

3 Neaten the border by cutting right round the edge of the bag, through both layers of fabric, with the pinking shears.

Hot-water Bottle
Cover

This must be the most complicated project in this book, but so worthwhile. The best thing about sewing projects is that once done, they are permanent fixtures and your efforts are much appreciated. This is such a very cosy thing for your guests to see lying on the bed on their arrival. Don't omit the piping – it absolutely 'makes' the overall design. Be sure that your fabric, piping and ribbon are washable.

Rectangle of wadding measuring 60 x 42cm (24 x 16¾in)

Rectangle of white cotton fabric measuring 60 x 42cm (24 x 16¾in)

Rectangle of main fabric measuring 60 x 42cm (24 x 16¾in)

Ruler

Pins

Template on page 126

45˚ set square

Matching sewing threads

Sewing machine with quilting guide

Two pieces of main fabric, cut to top-half template, plus 1.5cm (⅝in) seam allowance on bottom edge

One piece of white cotton lining, cut to bottom-half template, plus 1.5cm (⅝in) seam allowance on top edge

One piece of white cotton fabric cut to full template

Four pieces of 8mm- (½in-) wide ribbon, each measuring 16cm (6¼in) long

70cm (28in) of bias binding

70cm (28in) of no. 2 piping cord

Sewing needle

materials

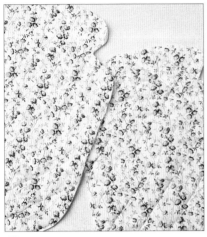

1 Lay the wadding on top of the white cotton fabric, then lay the main fabric on top of that. To machine-quilt the layers of fabric together in a diamond pattern, pin the layers together in the corners and the middle. Lay the set square in one corner and pin a diagonal line right across the fabrics. Machine along the line of pins, taking them out as you go. Set the quilting guide to 4cm (1½in) and, with it running along the first row of stitches, machine a second row. Continue in this way until you have worked right across the fabric, on both sides of the first line of machining. Repeat the process in the opposite direction to produce a diamond quilting pattern.

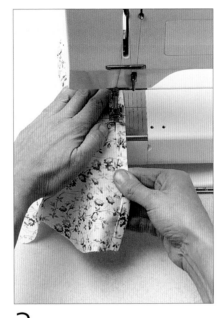

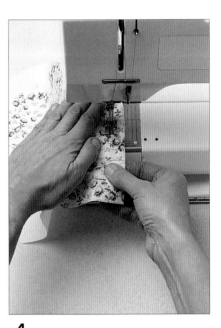

2 Enlarge the hot-water bottle cover template until it measures 40cm (16in) from top to bottom. Lay the template on one half of the quilted fabric and cut out a shape. Cut out another from the other half of the fabric. Set these aside and prepare the lining pieces.

3 On one of the top-half pieces of main fabric, turn over 0.5cm (¼in) then 1cm (½in). Machine close to the folded edge.

4 Right sides facing, machine the remaining top-half piece of the main fabric to the bottom-half piece of the white cotton fabric.

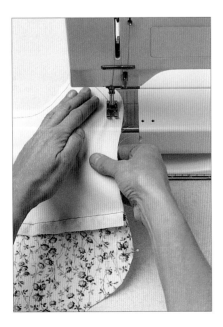

5 Right side up, lay the hemmed main-fabric top-half piece on to the right side of the white cotton full piece. Right side down, lay the joined main-fabric-and-lining piece on top of the hemmed main-fabric and white-lining pieces. Machine down the side from the shoulder point to just around the corner on the bottom edge. Repeat on the other side, so that the straight edge across the bottom is left open. Set the lining aside

6 On the quilted pieces, pin one end of a piece of ribbon to each side of the narrowest part of the neck.

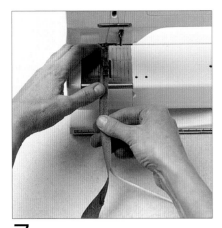

7 Using the bias binding and the piping cord, make up the piping. Simply open the binding out flat, place the cord in the middle of it and fold the binding in half over the cord. Machine close to the cord.

8 Pipe one of the quilted pieces from one shoulder point to the other. Start by neatening the end of the piping by clipping the cord back 1cm (½in) inside the bias binding, then folding the binding over the raw end of the cord. Machine the piping in place, 1.5cm (⅝in) in from the edge of the quilted fabric. Before you reach the other shoulder point, neaten the end as before.

9 With the piping foot still on the machine and right sides facing, machine the two quilted pieces together. Stitch as close as possible to the piping cord. Turn right side out.

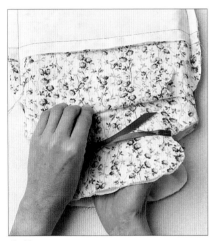

10 Right sides facing, slip the quilted section inside the lining section, aligning the top raw edges.

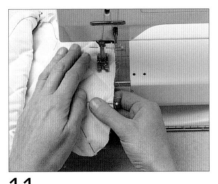

11 Machine round both top edges, catching in the pinned ends of the ribbon as you go. Trim the edges and clip the corners.

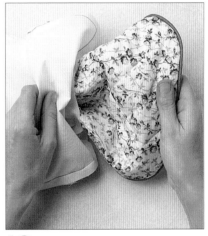

12 Ease the quilted section out through the gap in the bottom of the lining section.

13 Slip stitch the gap closed. Then push the lining inside the quilted section so that all the raw edges are concealed.

materials

Traycloth and napkin

Six-stranded embroidery thread (I used green, yellow and two shades of blue)

Embroidery needle

1 Either follow the design we have used (shown in detail below), or design your own flower arrangement. Using three strands of embroidery thread, embroider a small lazy-daisy-stitch flower in the corner of the napkin. Use two shades of a colour and vary the scale of the petals. After stitching each colour, leave the free end of the thread loose at the back, ready to move on to the next flower.

Traycloth and Napkin

Apart from looking gorgeous, a traycloth serves two very practical purposes: it stops the china from sliding around when you carry the tray and it also mops up any accidental spills. Embroidering a napkin to match completes the picture. Again, this is a project that can be done on your lap; the stitches are terribly easy and you can use whatever colours you want, to suit your china or guest bedroom.

2 Embroider another flower and stitch French knots between the petals.

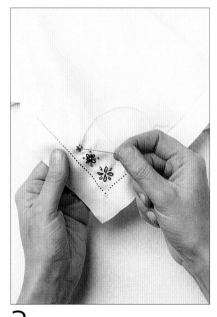

3 Stitch a yellow French knot in the middle of each flower.

4 Link the flowers with short lines of stem stitch.

Holding Parties

I simply adore planning parties and always look forward to them hugely. There are so many creative details to consider and make decisions upon – from invitations to menus, from themes to tablecloths. The more imagination you put into the planning, the more fun the party will be.

In this chapter we look at three different parties: a Halloween drinks party, a buffet for twenty people and a jolly party for pets and children.

Parties that revolve around a theme, such as Halloween, are a brilliant opportunity to go to town on decorations. We have carved a traditional Jack O'Lantern, with some contemporary details to give an original look. A light supper of soup and cheese biscuits is both delicious and fits in beautifully with the theme.

There is an emphasis on style for the buffet, so we have created table linen and napkin rings to give an elegant look to the event. In fact, we have made the same basic items for the pet party (see page 114); it just shows how different things can look if you add a little imagination.

Halloween
Party

At a party for both adults and children it is the children who need organized entertainment. The adults will be entertained by watching them and, to an extent, being involved in their games – a vicarious pleasure.

Theme parties, like Halloween, are ideal as they offer a relaxed atmosphere and some built-in fun. Most children, and many adults, love dressing up, especially if you can relate them to a character in a favourite book or film. Decorating the house is creative and really sets the scene and atmosphere for the guests as they arrive. There should, of course, be an emphasis on a 'friendly', rather than a 'spooky' Halloween, since one doesn't want to frighten younger children.

This is a party for fun and games, so prepare lots of fun things for the children to do in small groups. Rotate the groups so that everyone gets a go at everything.

Right: candles and lanterns give a wonderfully atmospheric light.

Left and below: this little witch was entranced by her trick-or-treat bag.

Planning
a Theme Party

A themed Halloween party is great fun for all ages and children are bound to be thoroughly over-excited about the whole occasion. They love to be involved in the planning and preparation of everything.

Rustic autumn colours make a welcome change from orange and black at Halloween. The tablecloths could be made of anything, but sacking looks wonderful and is inexpensive. Alternatively, you could make a jolly tablecloth using orange or white sheeting with potato-print moons and stars all over it (see page 122). Cut out paper shapes of pumpkins, witches, bats, stars, moons or maple leaves and hang them around the house (a row pegged to a piece of string like a washing line looks magical).

Setting the Scene

A collection of lanterns, or small paper bags weighed down with sand, with a night light in a jar inside, looks most effective. Use these to light the path to the house as well as inside. Put a pumpkin on either side of the front door to complement one inside (see page 100).

As people walk through the door, a 'welcome table' is gorgeous. Cover your sacking fabric with autumn leaves – maples or acers are particularly good for colour and shape. Offer everyone a drink – perhaps apple juice for children and a delicious spicy, mulled wine for the adults. The aroma of warm apples, oranges, cloves and cinnamon is particularly atmospheric.

Games to Play

There are many simple but fun games that children can play and that will keep them amused while the adults chat. These games will also serve to break the ice for children who haven't met before. Hold a costume competition, but give everyone a small prize for effort as well as a prize for the winner. Bobbing for apples is always hilarious – though I would suggest that witches and wizards remove their hats. Children particularly love it when adults have a go at this game as well. If you then suggest the children play 'Hunt the sweet in the plate of flour' immediately afterwards, you end up with some very funny, messy faces. They also love the challenge of eating a doughnut off a string without using their hands.

There is a good game involving the three senses of smelling, feeling and tasting. You pre-arrange four dark green bottles on a tray with straws; the children must guess what each liquid is, having tasted it through a straw. Then give them a cloth bag with four things in it; they must feel each thing and identify it. Then cover four jars and place a strong-smelling substance in each – eg soap powder, yeast extract, cheese, smoked mackerel – for them to sniff and identify.

A simple memory game is fun. Place ten or so objects on a tray and give the children one minute to memorize them. Then cover up the tray and ask them to list the items. Another idea for younger children is to present each child with a large greetings card that you have cut into about sixteen pieces with a guillotine. Give each child a piece of paper and ask them to piece the card back together like a jigsaw puzzle. Once in place, they can stick it down with a glue stick.

Children will be very thrilled to be presented with their very own, 'trick-or-treat' goodie bag (see page 102). You could even personalize these with their initial embroidered on the front. You may well have many of the same children to a party each year, so encourage them to keep their bags safely and bring them back. The bags also make a lovely going-home present.

Right: a tiny pumpkin, hollowed out and filled with flowers, makes a suitably seasonal vase.

• As much themed decoration as possible.

• Light food that is easy to eat.

• Drinks for both children and adults.

• Organized games for children to play.

checklist

CHEESE SCONES OR BISCUITS (makes about 10)

In a large bowl whisk 350g (12oz, 3 cups) of plain flour, 1tbsp baking powder, 1tbsp baking soda and 1tbsp salt together in a large bowl. Cut in 100g (4oz, ½ cup) of cubed butter until the mixture is crumbly. Then cut in 100g (4oz, ½ cup) of shortening and add 100g (4oz, ½ cup) finely chopped onion, 25g (1oz, ¼ cup) chopped parsley and 100g (4oz, 2 cups) of grated Cheddar cheese. Make a well in the centre and pour in ¾pt (400ml, 1½ cups) of buttermilk. Stir with a fork until the mixture comes together. Turn on to a floured board and knead. Pat the dough into a large round and cut out shapes. Put on a greased tray and bake at 200°C/400°F/gas mark 6 for 12-15min, until golden brown.

A Light Supper

Hot, pumpkin soup is popular with all ages. It has a unique taste and, if you want, you can add other root vegetables to its base to give it thickness and yet more flavour. To produce this soup in a big, hollowed-out pumpkin is hugely stylish, but be aware that it will cool down very quickly in a cold pumpkin; it is well worth warming up the empty pumpkin first in the oven. Serve the soup in mugs and garnish it with cream or sour cream, tiny bits of crispy bacon and chopped parsley.

Home-made Cheddar biscuits or scones are a fantastic accompaniment for this superb soup. You can, of course, make them in any shape you like, but these maple-leaf shapes are brilliant for Halloween. Serve them warm with a tiny knob of butter inside. (These also freeze and re-heat beautifully.) Cheese sables would also be utterly delicious but they are much more fragile to handle and serve and probably less suitable for children.

PUMPKIN SOUP
Cut a 1-1.5kg (2-3lb) pumpkin in half and scoop out all the seeds. Peel the pumpkin and cut it into small cubes. Sauté 5 peeled and chopped shallots and 2 crushed cloves of garlic in olive oil until transparent. Add 1tbsp of plain flour. Now add the cubed pumpkin, 2 large peeled and cubed potatoes and a little more olive oil or butter. Sauté for 5min. Add 600ml (1pt, $2^{1}/_{2}$ cups) of chicken stock, 600ml (1pt, $2^{1}/_{2}$ cups) of heavy cream, 600ml (1pt, $2^{1}/_{2}$ cups) of white wine, 2tsp of ground ginger and 2tsp of ground nutmeg. Cook until the vegetables are very soft then purée the soup.

Jack O'Lantern

Carving a pumpkin is a jolly project that all the family can take part in. Children can decide on the expression and draw it on, but an adult should do the actual carving. You do not want to do this more than a day before the event, as the cut edges will start to curl up. Our chilli-pepper ruff is very stylish, but you could go even further by using leaves or thin twigs for the hair or slices of mushroom for the eyebrows.

materials

Large, firm pumpkin

Water-based marker pen

Sharp kitchen knife

Long-handled spoon

Pins

Small carrot

100 green or orange chilli peppers

Darning needle

Fine string or button thread

1 Draw a lid shape around the stalk on the top of the pumpkin. Make a small key in the lid so that you can fit it back on again easily.

2 Cut through the drawn line with the sharp knife and lift the lid off. Wipe away any traces of the pen ink.

3 Scoop out the seeds and some of the flesh of the pumpkin with a spoon.

4 Either draw on the eyes or mark them out with pins.

Left: when Halloween is over, hang the strings of chillies up to dry, then use them again next year.

5 Cut out the eyes with the sharp knife. Always hold the pumpkin firmly and cut away from yourself.

7 Cut a small hole between the eyes to fit the fat end of the carrot. Wedge the carrot into the hole. If you can find an organic carrot with a curly tip, it makes a splendidly whimsical nose.

8 Thread the needle with 1m (39in) of string. Tie a knot in one end and thread on chilli peppers, just below the stalks. Don't touch your eyes and wash your hands afterwards as the chilli pepper juice is caustic.

6 Draw or mark out the mouth and cut it out in the same way.

9 Arrange the string of chillies in a double ruff around the base of the pumpkin. Only do this when the pumpkin is in its final position.

Rectangle of main fabric measuring 70 x 24cm (26 x 10in)

1m (39in) of cord

Ruler

Pins

Matching sewing thread

Sewing machine

Piece of lining fabric measuring 70 x 24cm (26 x 10in)

Scissors

80cm (31in) of 1cm- (½in-) wide velvet ribbon

Sewing needle

Two tassels with hanging loops

Two buttons

Trick or Treat Bag

This is the most charming item – appealing to any child. As with Christmas things, these can be stored to be used again year after year, or given to the children in the hope that they will bring them back next year. The mixture of textures is what gives them such appeal: a pumpkin button, combined with velvet ribbon, silky cord and sacking looks utterly wonderful. Experiment with your own combinations for other sumptuous effects. If you want bigger bags, increase the size by half and add a third button loop and button.

1 Machine each end of the length of cord to a long edge of the piece of main fabric, 1cm (½in) in and 16cm (6in) from one short edge.

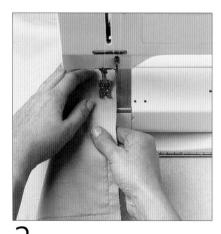

2 Right sides facing, machine the main fabric and lining together, taking a 1.5cm (⅝in) seam allowance and machining over the ends of the cord. Leave a gap in one long side.

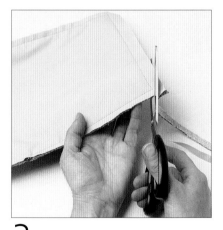

3 Clip the corners, then turn the bag right side out and slip stitch the gap closed. Press a fold in the fabric 27cm (10in) below the cord – this will be the bottom of the bag.

4 Pin each end of the ribbon on to the front flap of the bag, just below the cord. Leave 1cm (½in) of ribbon free at each end. Arrange the ribbon in a 'W' shape as shown, with two loops protruding over the end. These loops must be large enough to slip over the buttons you have chosen. Pin the ribbon in place then stitch it to the fabric along both sides.

5 At the ends of the ribbon, unpick a tiny section of the seam. Tuck the 1cm (½in) raw end of the ribbon into the gap and then stitch the seam closed, catching the ribbon into the stitches.

6 Trim the loops of the tassels to 2cm (¾in). Lay the cut ends on the lining, on the pressed bottom fold. Sew them to the lining with firm oversewing stitches.

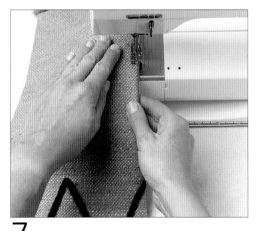

7 Fold the bag up at the bottom fold. Using a medium zigzag stitch, machine both the sides closed.

8 Fold the top flap of the bag down and sew on a button in line with each of the ribbon loops.

CHAPTER TEN

Buffet Party

A buffet is a wonderful way to entertain a large crowd in your house when you haven't got enough seating in your dining room alone. A buffet party also means that people can come and go since there is no formal seating, beginning or end to the party. If guests need to slip away early they won't be in danger of breaking up the party, nor will it be hugely noticed if they arrive a little late.

Even though it is a buffet, try to provide seating for everyone – use sofas, armchairs, bedroom, kitchen and garden chairs. Good seating adds to the greater comfort and relaxation of your guests. On top of this, you can commandeer every possible table or surface for drinks and plates – kitchen, nursery, card and garden tables all look fine with a cloth thrown over them. For the most elegant look, cover them all in identical tablecloths.

Planning a Buffet

Buffets are the natural solution to entertaining lots of people, either in the evening, or at lunchtime during weekends or holidays. It could be a special celebration or merely an excuse to have lots of fun without the worry of leaving anyone special out just because you can't squeeze any more around your dining-room table.

Glasses, drinks and ice can be laid in the hall for easy access and an instant welcome as your guests walk through the door (get them to put their coats in your prettiest bedroom upstairs or employ a willing child to be a 'coat minder'). A sideboard or large table can hold all the cutlery, napkins and food.

Seating Arrangements

Place chairs, in fours, around small tables, or put a table at each end of a sofa, with upright chairs opposite. Try to find enough seating for everyone: arms of sofas are uncomfortable and standing for hours is tiring. If it is a lunchtime buffet, you might put any children all together in the kitchen, where they can giggle and spill without any worries for you or them, or in the garden if the weather is fine: if you run out of chairs they will be happy on a rug. Be careful, however, never to let children feel second class in any way. Just as much trouble should be taken over their food, drink and general arrangements as you take for the adults.

- Enough chairs and tables for your guests
- Identical tablecloths for all the tables
- If possible, matching china and glassware
- Easily served and eaten food (see page 108)

checklist

Creating Stylish Tables

Identical tablecloths throughout will give your party an elegant look. Make them from an extremely inexpensive fabric with a small check, gentle stripe or floral print. Alternatively, plain sheeting, as we have used here, looks most effective; it is widely available and easy to sew and decorate. There are many ways of embellishing such simple fabric: ribbons and buttons are an obvious choice (see page 110). Make sure that the fabric you choose will go with your napkins. To make the napkin rings (see page 112) is a special touch and adds to the overall stylish effect. The wonderful thing is that all these pretty accessories, once made, can be stored away easily for the next party.

If you have managed to cajole your children into acting as waiters, so much the better. Ask them, as well as helping to serve food and drinks, to take empty plates and glasses out to the kitchen at regular intervals; this will keep the party room looking good and help to make the clearing up at the end so much easier. As thanks for their hard work, perhaps give each child an attractive reward.

Making Introductions

One of your roles as the hostess is to introduce people to one another so that everyone mixes and meets new people. It is a good idea to sit and think about your guests before the party begins. Think of people who have interests in common, whether it be a shared sport, similar job or children of the same age. This will give you a mental introduction list for the evening to help everyone enjoy themselves.

TOMATO CROUTES

Sweat 2 crushed garlic cloves and 1 finely chopped onion slowly in a little olive oil until very 'glassy'. Add 1 finely chopped fennel, 2 trimmed and finely chopped celery sticks, 1 tbsp tomato purée and 1 tin of chopped tomatoes. Simmer for 15min. Cut 4 slices of bread (without crusts) each into 16 tiny triangles. Drizzle them with olive oil and sprinkle with salt. Place on a metal tray and bake for 10min at 180°C/350°F/gas mark 4. Place a little of the tomato sauce on top of each croute. You can serve these warm or cold.

CHICKEN AND CUCUMBER SLICES

Mix mayonnaise with a little curry powder and pepper. Stir in finely chopped pieces of chicken. Cut slices of cucumber and pile a little chicken mayonnaise on each. Top with sprigs of dill.

Making Canapés

The starter must be some easy type of finger food. Attractive and easy to eat, canapés are perfect, but you must have napkins to hand. You don't have to offer many different kinds, but they should all vary in colour, shape and taste, and cater for vegetarians. There is an infinite variety to choose from – it entirely depends on what you feel like making. Another tempting alternative, which is extremely popular, is warm soup in a bone china mug, or in the summer; it could be a delicious iced soup.

FILO PRAWN TARTS
Make bite-size filo pastry cases in moulds; if you are able to buy ready-made ones, all the better. Combine shelled prawns, mayonnaise, Greek yoghurt, chopped dill and seasoning to make a fairly firm mix. Fill the cases at the last moment, as they go soggy quite quickly.

ASPARAGUS ROLLS
Trim then cook asparagus spears until just tender. Spread very thin slices of brown bread (without crusts) thinly with mayonnaise. Roll up each asparagus spear in a slice of bread.

It is best if the main course can be eaten without using a knife. An incredibly delicious meat or fish casserole would be perfect, as long as any meat is really tender and the sauce not is too runny. Salads are fine as long as the pieces in them are bite-size., Again, do consider any vegetarians. The sweet course is excellently served in individual ramekins – so neat and tidy.

Coffee, or herbal tea, to complete the meal, is always welcome. You may not have enough little cups and saucers, but no one minds mugs.

Ribboned Tablecloth

This is remarkably straightforward to make because all the machining is straight lines. Using sheeting is wonderfully economical and so practical when it comes to washing the tablecloth, but do check that your ribbon is washable, too. Using a wider version of the ribbon chosen to trim the napkin rings (see page 112) adds an extra stylish touch.

materials

Piece of sheeting the size of the finished tablecloth, plus 7.5cm (3in) on all sides

Pins

2.5cm- (1in-) wide ribbon, measuring twice the length and twice the width of the sheeting

Four 23mm (⁷⁄₈in) self-cover buttons

1 Turn under and press a 1cm (½in) then a 6.5cm (2½in) hem all round the sheeting.

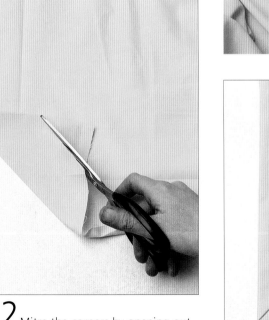

2 Mitre the corners by opening out the hems and pressing over a triangle. The centre of the base of the triangle should be at the point where the innermost pressed lines meet. Cut the pointed top off the triangle.

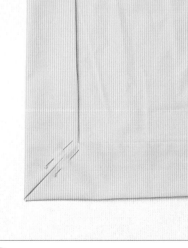

3 Refold the pressed hems and pin them in position.

4 Machine along all sides, stitching close to the pressed edge.

5 Lay the ribbon on the sheeting, with the bottom edge 4.5cm (1¾in) in from the edge of the fabric, so that the ribbon covers the line of machining. Pin it in place. At the corners, make a mitre by folding the ribbon over itself at right angles.

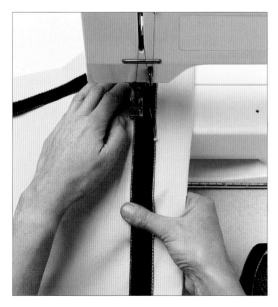

6 Machine the ribbon in place, stitching along both sides, close to the edges.

7 Cover the buttons by following the manufacturer's instructions. Sew one button to each of the mitred corners of the ribbon.

Rectangle of fabric measuring 10.5 x 17cm (4¼ x 6¾in)

Matching sewing threads

Sewing machine

Iron

23cm (9in) of 6mm- (¼in-) wide double-sided ribbon

Ruler

Pins

Sewing needle

Beading needle

Three large glass beads

Three tiny glass beads

Beaded Napkin Ring

You might think it would be tedious to produce quite so many napkin rings for a party, but, once made, they will always be there for all subsequent parties. There is only a small amount of machining involved so, again, lots of theraputic hand-sewing to do. The combination of the heavily textured yellow fabric with the satin ribbon and the glass beads is magical. The napkin rings look stunning in a heap and give the party such style.

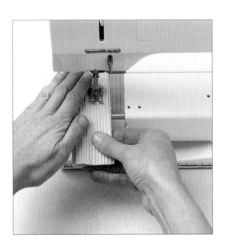

1 Right sides facing fold the fabric in half widthways and machine down one long side. Turn right side out, centre the seam at the back and press.

2 Measure and mark with a pin the halfway point on both edges of the fabric. On one edge, measure and mark 7cm (2¾in) either side of the halfway pin. On the other edge, measure and mark 3.5cm (1⅜in) either side of the halfway pin.

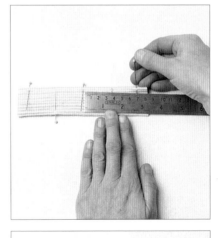

3 Zigzag the ribbon between the marked points, pinning it in place at the edges of the fabric.

4 Stitch the folds of the ribbon to the edge of the fabric with two tiny oversewing stitches.

5 Stitch a bead into the centre of the triangle formed by each ribbon zigzag. Take the thread up through the fabric, through the hole in the large bead then through the hole in the tiny bead.

6 Take the needle back down through the large bead and the fabric and pull the thread up tightly. The tiny bead will hold the large bead in place. Secure the thread at the back of the fabric.

7 Turn in and pin one raw end of the fabric, ensuring that the raw end of the ribbon is also turned. Tuck the other raw end into the turned end to form a circle. Ease the fabric in until the raw end of the ribbon is hidden, then adjust it so that the ends of the ribbon meet in a point. Pin in place.

8 Starting at the top on the inside of the ring, stitch the ends together. Slip stitch down the inside of the ring, then stitch up the outside.

Pet Party

When I was a child my mother always organized a party for our Pekinese's birthday. We adored it and Pollyanna, the Peke, seemed to as well.

Children identify very closely with their pets and a pet party is huge fun and produces instant entertainment for all those who attend. Involve the children as much as possible in all the planning and preparation: they will be terribly proud of what they have achieved on the day. However, not all animals respond well to this kind of party, so plan your guest list carefully. Make sure that both the invited children and parents understand the event and ask them not to bring nervous or argumentative animals along. Neither the animal nor the child will have much fun.

If the weather fails you, remember that children (and animals) usually don't mind getting wet – just put on waterproofs and carry on as planned.

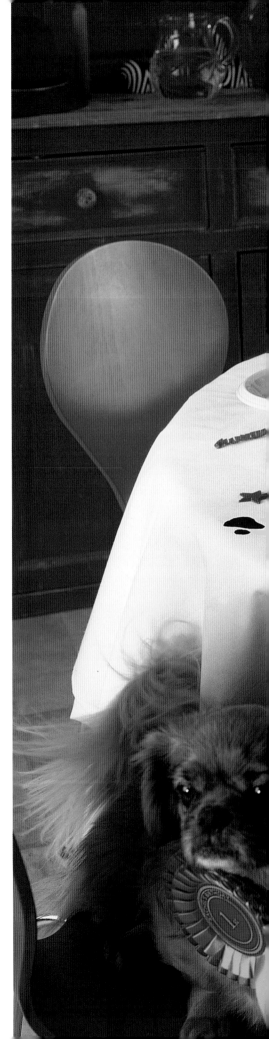

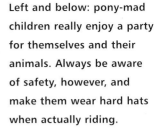

Left and below: pony-mad children really enjoy a party for themselves and their animals. Always be aware of safety, however, and make them wear hard hats when actually riding.

Planning for
Pets and Children

Either invite one type of pet only or animals that are known to get along with each other. A party that includes both cats and dogs is probably not such a good idea. Also, don't invite animals that are too big for the available space. Ponies make lovely guests, but if you have only a small garden, invite half-a-dozen dogs instead. If you are holding the party indoors, hamsters or guinea pigs are a better bet.

Send out the invitation cards with your pet as the host or hostess. Potato-print or stamp a motif onto the card. Alternatively, cut out pictures of happy-looking pets from a magazine or old birthday cards, or use photographs of your own pet and stick these on the card. Children love making these invitations and it conveys the theme of the party brilliantly. Personalized rosettes, either bought or home-made, are perfect as competition prizes for both dogs and ponies. Carry the theme through to the party table with rosette napkin rings (see page 120) and a printed tablecloth (see page 122).

A Pony Party

If your child is pony-mad and has friends with ponies, a pony party is not as difficult to arrange as it might sound. If you do not have enough space, you could always arrange the party on a local common, in a friend's field, at a riding stable or on a nearby beach. You need to be able to tie the ponies up, whatever happens; string loops around trees, fence posts or horseboxes would be fine. Tie the ponies well apart when you are not riding them, to avoid any kicking or biting. Haynets could be brought to keep them happy.

Left and below left: bundles of carrots or biscuits make great going-home presents for pets.
Below: invitations to fit the theme of the party don't have to be complicated; this is just a potato print on card.

The following gymkhana games are exciting and don't require too much advance preparation:

Potato Race – canter up to a bucket. Dismount. Take a potato out of the bucket. Remount. Canter back and drop it into another bucket.

Above: Beryl loves parties, particularly ones where lots of delicious food is on offer.

Bending Race – ride in and out of four poles and back again.

Mug Race – put up four poles, with a mug on poles one and three. The rider must move the mugs to poles two and four respectively.

If you are really involved with horses, you can set up a course or hire some jumps from your local riding stable and hold a mini show jump. Plan a dressage test and mark out an arena for the children to perform it in. A best-turned-out child and pony or fancy-dress competition can also be fun. It depends on how much space you have and how far you want to go. An ideal going-home present for ponies is two or three carrots tied up with colourful ribbon. The ponies will be thrilled.

A Dog Party

If it is a dog party it's best if the dogs arrive on leads; they can then be let loose in the garden to get to know each other. Dogs usually respond well to organized events, so set up a jumping course with boxes and broomhandles and get everyone, children and dogs alike, to go round it. You could also arrange a running race for the dogs – on or off their leads. Mark out a little show ring and hold a competition. Choose whimsical classes that any dog could win, such as: dog with the waggiest tail; dog most like its owner; dog the judge would most like to take home. Make sure there are lots of bowls of water around – dogs get so thirsty when they are rushing about. Give each dog two chew-sticks, tied together with checked ribbon, as a going-home present.

- Enough space for the animals you want to invite to the party.
- Enough tying-up places for all the ponies.
- Plenty of bowls of water for dogs.
- Games to play that everyone can join in.

checklist

Party Food

EGG MAYONNAISE ISLANDS
Mix some mayonnaise in a bowl with ⅓ of the same amount of Greek yoghurt. Add seasoning and mashed hard-boiled eggs. Spoon on to thinly sliced rounds of French bread.

Choose typical children's party food – finger food that is small and easy to handle – for this party. Check if any of the children coming have any allergies or special diets and cater for them, too. It is really sad for a child if they are left out of any aspect of a party.

The food must be attractive in colour and varied in flavour and taste. Give some thought to the food presentation so it all looks very edible, then you won't have heaps of left-overs. There should be lots of savoury food so that they fill up on that before moving on to the sweet things. Sweets look so enticing in little bowls for small fingers to dip in and out of and children also love chocolate crispie or cornflake cakes. Offer both fruit juices and fizzy drinks to accompany the food.

SESAME-SEEDED SAUSAGES
Roast sausages in a hot oven (200°C/400°F/gas mark 6) for about 20min. Put them in a bowl and spoon over a little runny honey to make them sticky all over. Shower them with toasted sesame seeds. Serve warm with napkins near at hand.

CHOCOLATE CRISPIES

Melt 75g (3oz, ⅓ cup) of butter and 100g (4oz, ⅓ cup) of syrup in a large saucepan. Once melted, remove from the heat and stir in 100g (4oz, 4 squares) of chocolate, broken into small pieces. When completely melted, add 150g (5oz, 1¾ cups) of crisped breakfast cereal and stir until thoroughly combined. Spoon into paper cases. Place in the fridge for at least 1hr, or 20min in the freezer if in a hurry.

materials

60cm (24in) of 2.5cm- (1in-) wide ribbon

Scissors

Matching sewing thread

Sewing needle

Iron

Ruler

15cm (6in) of 1cm- (½in-) wide ribbon

Pins

Circle of gold card measuring 3cm- (1¼in-) diameter

PVA glue

Pen

Rosette Napkin Ring

These would amuse children no end and emphasize the theme of the party famously. They are also a fun item for the children to take home at the end of the day as a souvenir. They are not difficult to make and can comfortably be assembled in your lap in your lap. You could make them in lots of different colours or just one, as I have here.

1 Cut the length of 2.5cm- (1in-) wide ribbon in half and stitch a line of small running stitches close to one edge of one piece.

2 Pull the gathers up tightly and stitch the raw ends together at the back to form a rosette.

3 Press the rosette flat.

4 Cut the remaining 30cm (12in) of 2.5cm- (1in-) wide ribbon into one 14cm (5½in) and one 16cm (6½in) piece. Fold each piece in half widthways and pin it with the point of the pin towards one end. Cut this end in a diagonal from the edge to the centre, so that when you open it out it forms a 'V' shape.

5 Lay the ends of the 1cm- (½in-) wide ribbon together to form a loop. Pin the loop to the top back of the gathered edge of the rosette and stitch it in place. Turn 2cm (1in) of the raw end of the longer piece of wide ribbon over the raw end of the shorter piece. Pin the pieces to the back of the rosette, on top of the loop stitching, and stitch them in place.

6 Glue the card circle into the centre of the front of the rosette. Write each child's initial on the card circle of their rosette.

materials

Sheeting large enough to
cover your table, or an old
bed sheet

Matching sewing thread

Sewing machine

Paw-print template on
page 126

Large potato cut in half

Craft knife

Sharp kitchen knife

Fabric paint

Foam roller

Plate

Paw-print Tablecloth

This could be a project entirely done by children: they can go and find
a completely non-special sheet in the linen cupboard, make the potato
print (though they may need help cutting it out if the knife is sharp)
and then print the tablecloth. I made this cloth from sheeting and
stamped it with doggy paw prints, but you could stamp on any other
simple shape – horseshoes look very good.

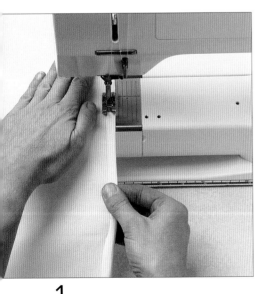

1 Make a narrow double hem round
all sides of the sheeting. If you are
using an old sheet, you may have to
cut it down to size and hem any raw
edges.

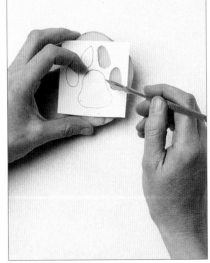

2 Enlarge the template to the
required size, making sure that it will
fit on your potato. Lay the template
on the potato and cut out the paw
print with a craft knife, cutting
through the paper into the potato.

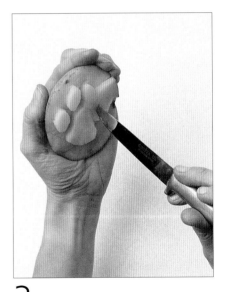

3 Remove the template and with a
sharp kitchen knife, cut out the paw
print. You need to remove about
0.5cm (¼in) in depth of potato
around each element of the design.

4 Put some fabric paint on an old plate. Roll the roller through the paint and then on to the cut-out paw print.

5 Press the potato down on to the sheeting to stamp the design on it.

6 Stamp rows of paw prints across the cloth, as if your dog had taken a stroll across it with very muddy feet.

Templates

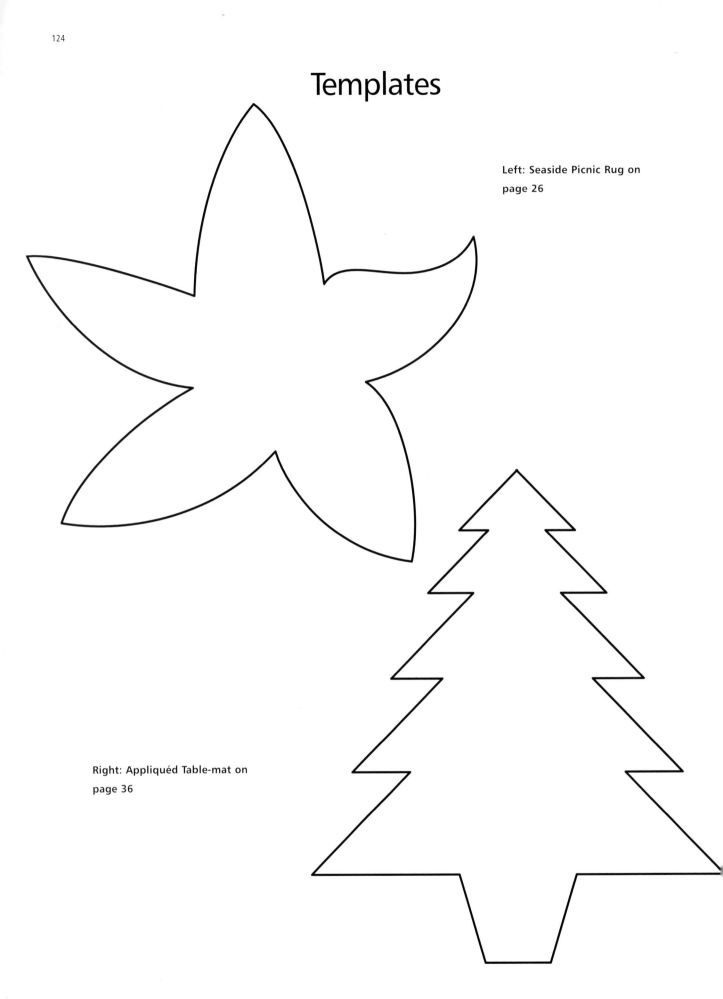

Left: Seaside Picnic Rug on page 26

Right: Appliquéd Table-mat on page 36

**Above and right: Laundry Bag
on page 78**

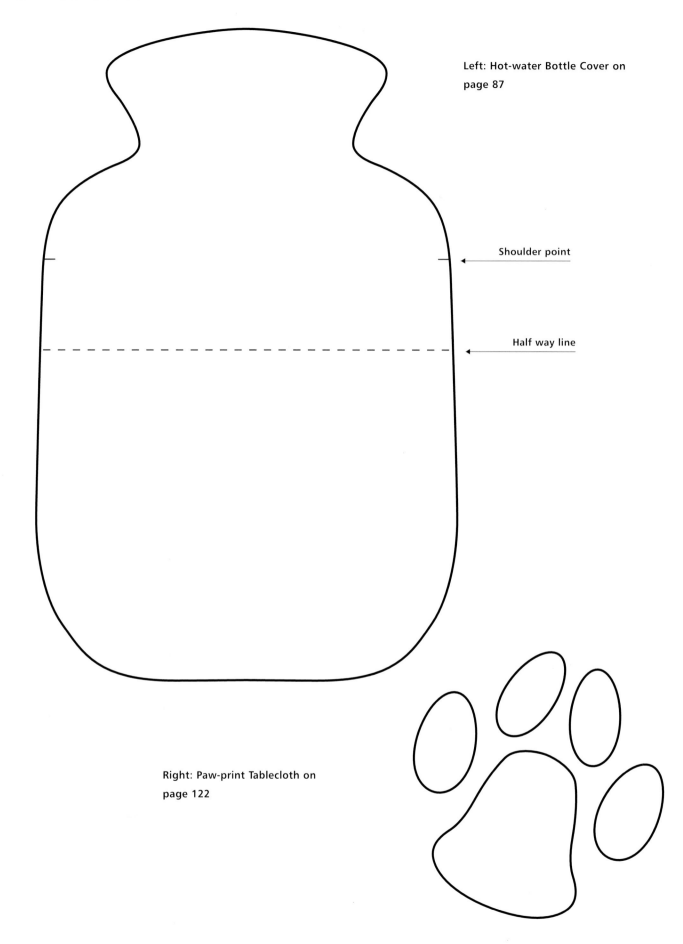

Left: Hot-water Bottle Cover on
page 87

Shoulder point

Half way line

Right: Paw-print Tablecloth on
page 122

Author's Acknowledgements

I would like to thank all my family for their continuing interest and enthusiasm over the production of my books, which they know give me enormous pleasure to write. I am so grateful to Cameron Brown and to Colin Zeigler, my publishers, for their huge support of my work.

I could not do these books without Kate Haxell, my freelance editor, who is just fantastic at making a project happen, or else developing one into something brilliant. She has terrific flair and focus for everything creative. I also want to thank Kate Kirby, my in-house editor, who kindly continues to believe in me and is equally supportive over each new book. Thank you also to Lucinda Symons for her fabulous style photography, which is unbeatable, and to Brian Hatton for his wonderful food photography and extremely diligent step-by-step pictures. Their two assistants, Emma and Holly, were totally invaluable, too.

I want to thank Alastair Turnbull for his brilliant styling which has 'made' the book and to thank Janet James for her highly skilled book design. Thank you to Sonia Pugh for her hard work in marketing my books and also to Pam Wardly for her marvellous and invaluable sewing help with many of the projects. Her assistant, Pat Hembrow, was also wonderful.

Publisher's Acknowledgements

Collins & Brown would like to thank the following companies for loaning props for photography:

Christophe (020 7491 4004), formal glassware and cutlery.

Cologne and Cotton (020 7376 0324), bedlinen.

Purves & Purves (020 7580 8223), furniture.

The Pier (020 7637 7001), informal tableware, glassware and accessories.

Wedgewood (0800 317 412), formal tableware.

For curtain-making equipment, including fabric clamps, folding rulers, small metal rulers, long pins and long needles, or if you would like to have any of the projects in this book made to order, contact Caroline Wrey at:

66 Mysore Road
London SW11 5SB
Tel: 020 7738 2036
Fax: 020 7787 0419

Index